The Rutledge Book of
BASEBALL

The Rutledge Book of
BASE

By Bill Conlin

The Rutledge Press
New York, New York

445

Edited by Deborah Weiss
Designed by Allan Mogel

Copyright © 1981 by The Rutledge Press

All rights reserved. No part of this book
may be reproduced or transmitted in any
form or by any means, electronic or mechanical,
including photocopying, recording or by
any information retrieval system, without
permission in writing from the Publisher.

Published by The Rutledge Press
A Division of W.H. Smith Publishers Inc.
112 Madison Avenue, New York, New York 10016

First printing 1981
Printed in Hong Kong

ISBN 0-8317-7596-3

Library of Congress Cataloging in Publication Data

Conlin, Bill.
    The Rutledge book of baseball.

    1. Baseball—United States—History. I. Title.
GV863.A1C596   796.357'0973   81-5197
                                        AACR2

Contents

1

The Babe, Jackie, Charlie O., and Curt

In 1920, most of the boys were back from Over There, all but the ones who found permanent residence in the Argonne, the St. Mihiel salients, and other killing grounds that have faded into history. All came home but the ones helping the British and French occupy the Rhineland, or those who had gone to the Ukraine to fight the dreaded Bolsheviks.

In 1920, the booming economy of wartime was turning soft. America would shortly plunge into a brief but devastating mini-depression, brought on by the inability of prostrate Europe to buy our flood of mass-produced manufactured goods. Early in the first year of the decade, the average hourly wage earned by U.S. workers was 50 cents an hour. For $125,000 a citizen of 1920 could buy 832,000 pounds of hamburger. Or 192.3 Ford automobiles. Or the services for one hour of 250,000 factory workers.

And if a 1920 American wished to achieve ultimate status as an entrepreneur, he could buy a famous baseball player named George Herman Ruth.

This is what a New York City beer baron named Jake Ruppert did on a January afternoon. Ruppert purchased the game's most famous player from the financially strapped Boston Red Sox for $125,000. It was big enough news to make people briefly forget about the newly sworn Republican president, Warren G. Harding, food riots and rampant anarchy in Germany, and federal enforcement of the Volstead Act, soon to be the law of what was supposed to be a dry land.

The sale of Ruth to the Yankees marked the first great turning point for major league baseball. Ruth gave the public a national sports hero to lionize. If Charles Lindbergh emerged as the most admired figure of the Roaring Twenties, Ruth was the undisputed chairman of the fun and games department. He was made for the decade—a loud, profane glutton of a man who burned his candle at both ends. The Babe was suspended by Judge Kennesaw Mountain Landis, the czar the owners appointed to police the game in the wake of 1919's notorious betting scandal. He was involved in headline-grabbing salary disputes, missed time with gargantuan hangovers, and dominated the sport until his sad, hanging-on-for-a-payday decline in 1935.

But Babe Ruth was a hero of white America, a nation where blacks were suppressed by the demeaning facts of economic and social segregation. Jackie Robinson came to the majors in 1947, two years after the conclusion of an even bloodier world war, when "separate but equal" was still a cynical fact of life in the southern states and an unwritten practice in the rest of the nation. There was no civil rights law on the federal books. Whether by state statutes or by pro forma intimidation, blacks were disenfranchised.

Professional baseball was as white as the pure-driven snow. Apartheid in the sport had been formalized in 1867, two years after the end of the fratricidal war which ended slavery. The National Association of Baseball Players met in the "cradle of liberty," Philadelphia, and ruled that clubs that employed blacks would be barred. The association folded and its successor, the National Association of Professional Baseball Players—still in existence as the minor league governing body—carried on the ban in the form of an unwritten understanding.

By the 1880's several "Negro" leagues were thriving and at least 20 blacks were performing for semipro and minor league teams. It remained for Adrian Constantine ("Cap") Anson to utter the words that kept the major leagues lily white until 1947.

Anson, manager of the Chicago White Stockings, was a brilliant player and a notorious racist. The Toledo club of the American Association had signed two black players, Moses Fleetwood Walker and his brother William Wellday Walker. Before a game in Toledo in 1887, Anson saw Walker warming up with his teammates. "Get that nigger off the field," Anson thundered and said he would pull his team off the field if Walker didn't leave the ball park. Walker stayed, Anson backed down, and the game was played.

Anson later created such a flap that a trade

Pages 2–3: *What the batter sees at Chicago's Comiskey Park.*
Pages 6–7: *The World Series, 1980, Royals Stadium.*

which would have brought a black player, Newark's George Stovey, to the New York Giants was aborted. Major league baseball thus plunged itself into 60 years of stony sleep.

On a steamy morning in August 1945, just days after 100,000 Japanese were incinerated by a new type of bomb dropped by a single B-29, a recently discharged army officer named Jack Roosevelt Robinson walked into the Montague Street offices of the Brooklyn Dodgers. Following a long and exhaustive investigation of his background and character, Branch Rickey, the innovative and intellectually brilliant president and majority owner of the National League club, decided the former UCLA three-letter man could handle the awesome breakthough.

Rickey knew Jackie Robinson could hit. Hell, his scouts had handed him a long list of Negro League stars who met all the physical requirements. There was a catcher named Roy Campanella with power equal to the legendary Josh Gibson. There was a tall, right-handed pitcher named Don Newcombe with a fastball that trailed sparks. There was a veteran Negro League star named Monte Irvin sure to hit .300 in the majors and certified sluggers named Larry Doby and Luke Easter. Rickey also had a list of Latin prospects whose skins happened to be black.

But Rickey wanted a black good enough to dispel forever the popular myth that, "a nigger could never make it playing in the big leagues," disciplined enough to turn the other cheek early and often and possessed of high enough moral standards to stay out of trouble off the field.

All the Dodgers impresario wanted was a cross between Josh Gibson, Uncle Remus, and Caesar's wife. Although Rickey's humanitarian motives were sincere, it would be a mistake to assume that the bible-quoting, proverb-spouting attorney was bucking for a place in history next to Abraham Lincoln. Rickey also had an eagle eye for a dollar, and certain socioeconomic factors were obvious to him as World War II came to a close. An unprecedented northward migration had taken place during the war. The industrial cities of the Northeast and Middle Atlantic states from Baltimore to Boston had acquired significant black populations. Blacks came to work in defense plants and war-related industries. Or they merely wished to escape the thralldom of life in the rural South. Whatever, they would be staying, multiplying, and would become a major force in the urban economy. And wherever the first black major league player appeared, this vi-

tal new force in city life would flock to root their brother across the frontier of baseball's brave new world.

The meeting between the proud young black man and the shrewd old baseball man was a classic.

"Suppose they throw at your head?"

"Mr. Rickey, they've been throwing at my head a long time."

"It's an important ball game and in the heat of it I collide with you at second base. I jump up and yell, 'You dirty black bastard!' What do you do then?"

"Mr. Rickey, do you want a player who's afraid to fight back?"

Rickey pointed a pudgey finger at Robinson.

"I want a ballplayer with guts enough not to fight back. You're in a World Series game and I'm a hot-head. I spike you but you don't give ground. I jump up and you stand there jabbing the ball in my ribs and the umpire yells, 'Out!' All I can see is that black face, so I punch you in the cheek. What do you do?"

Rickey finished his superb performance by throwing a mock punch that missed Robinson's chin by inches. The enormity of what Rickey was asking him to do had finally sunk in.

A trace of bitterness flickered briefly across Robinson's face. Then he relaxed.

"I've got two cheeks," he said. "Is that it?"

"Yes," Rickey said.

It was the second great turning point of modern baseball. At last, the national pastime was open to all the citizens of the nation. In Babe Ruth the game had a towering figure for future stars to be measured against, the Greenbergs, DiMaggios, Williamses, Musials, Kiners, Aarons, and Schmidts; the Mantles, Marises, Clementes, Fosters, and Garveys. Robinson was a linchpin for a tremendous surge of blacks and Latins who upgraded the game and added a new dimension to it—sheer, unbridled speed of foot.

It remained for an insurance hustler from Chicago to put a battering ram to some of baseball's yeasty traditions, propelling it into the 1980s wearing colorful new garments and with a bold new rule.

The man was Charles O. Finley. O. for outrageous, outlandish, obstreperous, ostentatious, obscene, or as in, "I am the Owner."

Until Finley jumped feet-first into baseball when he bought out Kansas City owner Arnold Johnson in 1961, there was only one broad, distinct breed of owner—the well-heeled shorthairs. By and

large they were gentlemen-sportsmen and were personified by men like Boston Red Sox owner Tom Yawkey, Chicago Cubs owner Philip K. Wrigley, Philadelphia Phillies owner Bob Carpenter, and St. Louis beer baron August Busch.

These men loved the game and were independently wealthy from other sources. Wrigley was a chewing-gum heir, Carpenter a DuPont scion, Yawkey a construction tycoon. They were paternalistic figures who also knew a tax write-off when they saw one. Few owners were in major league baseball to make a substantial profit and few did.

On the big-business Richter scale, major league baseball is a minor tremor in the marketplace. Even in 1980 all the assets of the 26 franchises would barely nudge baseball into the *Fortune* (magazine) 500. And no self-respecting entrepreneur would operate on the game's slim profit margins. For example, the 1979 Phillies drew a club record 2.75 million fans to Veterans Stadium, the National League's premier facility. Despite rev-

enues of more than $12 million, the club claims it lost money. Be aware that no major league team has ever been required to open its books to the public. Creative accounting is possible because of factors like depreciation of the assets—the players—and deferred salaries, which run into the twenty-first century. But the fact remains, in a year of peak interest and prosperity, the Phillies did not make a significant amount of money.

One exception to the gentleman-sportsman makeup of the fraternity was a maverick named Bill Veeck, who was more a promoter of shabby ballclubs over the years than a successful owner. At one time or another, Veeck was a managing partner of the impoverished St. Louis Browns, Chicago White Sox, and Cleveland Indians.

Veeck was a baseball-loving speculator with little cash of his own who was always able to round up a syndicate of stockholders to bankroll the operation. A more spectacular exception to the millionaire-owner was Walter O'Malley, a Brooklyn

Opposite: *George Herman Ruth, "the Sultan of Swat." Babe's power and charisma gave a weary America someone to cheer.* Above: *Jackie Robinson gives his farewell address. Robinson broke the color barrier and ended in the Hall of Fame.*

attorney who handled the affairs of the Dodgers and eventually purchased the majority stock in the club from Branch Rickey. When the Brooklyn Borough Council dragged its feet over constructing a facility to replace decaying Ebbets Field, O'Malley joined forces with Giants owner Horace Stoneham. In a move that was as inevitable as Robinson's crossing of the color line, O'Malley moved the Dodgers to Los Angeles and Stoneham set up shop in San Francisco.

Through shrewd manipulation, the O'Malley family today owns the most profitable operation in the game's history. The Dodgers hold the mortgage to their splendid stadium in Chavez Ravine, regularly draw more than 2.5 million free-spending fans, and have twice topped the magic 3 million mark. O'Malley became the first baseball owner to become a millionaire from profits generated by the game itself.

Finley made a modest fortune in the midwest selling malpractice insurance plans to the medical profession. But he had a much bigger ego than the successful sale of insurance could satisfy. Finley craved attention and he became the most controversial owner in baseball history, a man who received more publicity than his most famous players—Reggie Jackson, Jim ("Catfish") Hunter, and Vida Blue. He wrote the rules as he went along and bent them to suit his needs. Although he went into club ownership with a clear eye for profit, Finley left a broad swath of red ink in his wake. His motto could have been, "Have baseball team, will travel."

After unsuccessful attempts to move the Kansas City franchise to Louisville and Dallas-Ft. Worth, Finley finally won approval to set up shop across the Bay from Stoneham's struggling team in the blue-collar city of Oakland. He was a carpetbagger in the truest sense of the word. But he will not be remembered for an ill-advised move to a market which was barely supporting one team.

Charles O. Finley dragged the game, kicking and screaming, into the twentieth century. He is the iconoclast who brought us the designated hitter (DH) rule used everywhere but in the National League. He is responsible for midweek playoff and World Series games being played at night during prime television viewing time. He brought us the multihued, form-fitting double-knit uniforms that have replaced the traditional white or gray flannel sacks.

Finley, a man with scant prior baseball experience, spurned the traditional way of running a major league franchise. His colleagues scoffed when he announced he would be his own general manager, make his own trades, and sign most of his own talent. The lords of baseball stopped laughing when Finley assembled a dynasty that dominated the game through the mid-1970s. He ran through field managers the way Mickey Rooney runs through wives. He outraged the Establishment by letting his mule mascot, the late, great Charley O., wander undiapered through the Oakland Stadium hospitality room during World Series parties. He dressed his athletes in white shoes topped by a green, white, and gold ensemble.

"There is no there there," Gertrude Stein once said of Oakland. But Finley put the factory and shipyard town on the baseball map. His teams won five straight Western Division titles. They won the World Series in 1972, 1973, and 1974. Although the patient was a success, the operation died. The Athletics drew more than a million fans only twice.

Sixteen managers were hired and fired by Finley before he sold the A's to an Oakland syndicate of clothing manufacturers in the summer of 1980. The Phillies and Dodgers employed more people to sell their tickets than he hired to run an entire organization. When fans failed to get calls through the switchboard in the club offices, the standing joke was that the telephone operator was busy running the elevator. Finley was a gaudy, irreverent Napoleon leading a phantom army. His constant Waterloo was Commissioner Bowie Kuhn, a patrician lawyer from Princeton, New Jersey. The highlight of Finley's many confrontations with Kuhn, who often represented how a majority of the owners were thinking, came when the commissioner vetoed his attempt to sell Jackson, Blue, and Joe Rudi for $3.5 million. The sale, Kuhn ruled, would enable the Yankees and other wealthy clubs to buy championships and, therefore, upset the game's competitive balance.

Finley responded by slapping Kuhn and major league baseball with a $12 million antitrust suit. But the courts ruled that Kuhn had acted within the scope of his powers.

Finley's motto was, "Sweat plus sacrifice equal success." Many who worked for him figured they were providing the sweat and sacrifice while Charley enjoyed the success. A man who demanded long hours and deep loyalty, Finley led the majors in thrift. If it was your long-distance phone call, he would expound for hours. If it was his, he used a three-minute egg timer.

"Sometimes he treats black players like

damned niggers," Vida Blue once groused after a go-round with his owner. "That's okay," a team-mate replied. "Charley treats white players like niggers, too."

Finley always thought one of the great wastes in baseball was permitting pitchers to hit. Why, he asked at every owners' meeting, should an inept offensive performer be permitted to drag down a club's run production when a hitting specialist could be inserted in his place?

Sheer heresy! Finley's colleagues would have had him burned as a witch if the year had been 1574 instead of 1974. Why, he asked, should an aging star whose legs and fielding reflexes were gone but who could still swing a bat be put out to pasture? After years of bullying and agitating at league meetings, Finley got his way. The DH rule was adopted by the American League, and although the National League has held firm, the rule was narrowly defeated by a 5–4 margin in 1980, with three teams abstaining. Even staunch DH foes feel the rule will be adopted by the National League no later than the 1982 season.

People laughed when Finley unveiled form-fitting uniforms in glaring colors he fondly called, "Kelly green, California gold, and Polar Bear white." To some, the A's looked like a company softball team ready for combat in a beer league. But women loved the colorful raiment and the sexy cling, and at least one rival owner grudgingly admitted, "They may not be baseball uniforms but they're damn good looking."

All 26 big league teams have gone to the cooler, lighter, more efficient double-knits. Only two, the Yankees and Dodgers, still wear the traditional gray of the road uniform.

Finley didn't stop with the DH rule and the jet-age uniform. He lobbied for orange baseballs for better fan and TV visibility. He pushed for a walk to be awarded after a pitcher threw three balls. During the 1974 season he signed Herb Washington, a slender Olympic sprinter, and announced that soon teams would have a designated runner to go with their DH. Finley quietly dropped that scheme when Washington's baserunning blunders helped cost the A's a defeat in the World Series.

White baseballs and the four-ball walk are likely to be with us through the eighties. But Finley had made his point. There was room in the game for change, and a good game could not bind itself to nineteenth-century traditions.

Finley kept hammering at Kuhn and the owners to permit the TV networks to air midweek post-season games in prime time. Baseball was showcasing its championship games in time reserved for soap operas, he said. If baseball expected lush TV paydays, the sport would have to fit itself into the top advertising-dollar time slots. When it came to money, the opposition to night postseason games was lukewarm. Ironically, the first World Series night game was played in Oakland in 1973. A freak hail-and-rain storm enveloped Oakland-Alameda County Stadium shortly before game time, the historic event was postponed, and 500 baseball writers whose deadlines had been savaged by the late start wrote pointedly that it didn't rain during that day in Oakland. While the live studio audience sits in driving rain and bone-chilling cold, the World Series will continue to be played for the benefit of Armchair America. (Don't ask a baseball owner if he would sacrifice the quality of the game for a nine-figure TV contract.) Charles O. Finley showed them the way.

Babe Ruth put baseball on the national map, turning away with his talent and charisma the wrath and distrust caused by the Black Sox scandal. Jackie Robinson integrated it. Charles O. Finley streamlined baseball at a time when pro football was threatening to surpass it as the American game. It remained for a gifted, articulate black outfielder named Curt Flood to start the legal process that eventually overturned the reserve system that bound a player to the club that owned his contract for life, or until he was unconditionally released.

The National League was born in 1876. Four years later, the Cincinnati club was drummed from the corps for playing baseball on the sabbath and failing to discourage the consumption of hard liquor at games. As a result of that divorce, Cincinnati owner Justin Throner and H.D. Knight of Pittsburgh founded the American Association and all hell broke loose. The new league undercut the National's ticket prices by 50 percent, played games on Sunday, and raided its rivals unscrupulously. Out of chaos came the National Agreement. A clause aimed at preventing players from jumping from team to team and league to league was written into player contracts.

The American League was founded in 1901. After two years of franchise juggling, the "major leagues" arrived at a geographical alignment that would endure until 1953, when the Boston Braves received permission to move to Milwaukee. The reserve system was the solid rock in which the game's foundation was imbedded. The system was based on several sentences in the standard player contract

which, in effect, bound a player to the club that owned the contract, with almost no reservations. The clause permitted a player to be traded, without his permission, to any other major league club. A player's only hope to make a deal for himself was through an unconditional release. And when a player was released it was a signal to all parties that he was too infirm, too old, or too unskilled to continue at the top level of the game.

This autocratic control of employee by employer was a clear violation of the antitrust laws, but Congress had traditionally cited the "unique nature of the sport" in any attempt to bring baseball under the legal umbrella which covered business in the real world.

Defenders of the reserve clause held that rigid measures of control were needed to keep the wealthy teams from signing the best players and creating a competitive imbalance—something the Yankees had managed to do legally for four decades. What the system's proponents really meant was that, while they could live with the Yankees in the World Series most years, the game would be destroyed by the escalation in salaries a free market would bring as clubs bid for the game's stars. This philosophy became known as, "The best interests of the game," a phrase which recurs whenever the owners are threatened with financial disruption. (It was invoked to the letter by Kuhn when he voided Finley's $3.5 million player sale.)

Above: *Curt Flood, the first player to challenge the owner-dictated reserve clause.* Opposite: *Jim ("Catfish") Hunter finished what Flood started, successfully suing Charles O. Finley for free-agent status.*

So the reserve clause hung over the hired help like a sword of Damocles. It was wielded by Judge Landis when he barred the Black Sox fixers for life, even though they were never found guilty in a court of law. It was wielded by Commissioner Happy Chandler when he suspended several players who jumped to the Mexican League in 1947, hardly a heinous crime.

In October 1969, Flood, then 32 and in the prime of a fine career, was informed by the Cardinals that he had been traded to the Phillies in a multi-player transaction. Flood was stunned. He had served the Cardinals well for 12 seasons. What really disturbed the outfielder was that they could banish him to a city where he had no desire to play. Shouldn't he be able to offer his services around, have something to say about a decision that would profoundly affect his entire family? The Phillies felt his reaction to the trade was typical. Once over the initial shock of being treated like heads of cattle, most players packed their bags and moved on. The language of their contracts left them with only one other choice. That was to quit baseball and go into another line of work. When an IBM employee is transferred from Los Angeles to a less desirable city, he is left with certain options. He can apply for a job with a rival corporation.

Where can a .285 hitter who does not wish to move to Philadelphia find an equivalent market for his skills? There are only two major leagues and both play by the same set of rules.

Flood refused the trade, even though the Phillies offered him a then-handsome $100,000 contract. The Establishment viewed Flood's recalcitrance as a ploy to bleed a few more dollars out of the Phillies. The owners recoiled in shock and horror when Flood hired former Supreme Court Justice Arthur J. Goldberg and announced he would go toe-to-toe with the Lords of baseball. Before taking that giant step, Flood conferred with Marvin Miller, executive director of the increasingly powerful Major League Players Association. Flood told Miller he wanted to sue baseball on constitutional grounds, that he wanted to give the courts a chance to overturn the reserve clause. Miller outlined the difficulties. Win or lose, Flood would wear the bell of a leper. He could forget about managing or holding a baseball job when his playing days were over. The legal costs would be enormous and the suit could drag for years through the courts while time stole his remaining baseball skills. Worse, Miller said, Flood stood a helluva chance of losing. The outfielder said he was aware

15

of the consequences and wished to proceed. Flood received the unanimous blessing of the Players Association.

There would be no turning back, Flood told Goldberg. Once the legal machinery was in motion he would go all the way. There would be no question of his settling out of court the way Danny Gardella had in 1949.

Gardella, one of the Mexican League jumpers, sued baseball and won his action in a Federal Appeals Court. But rather than endure a baseball counter-appeal, Gardella settled out of court and the reserve clause remained a de facto part of the standard player contract. Flood was determined to go all the way to the Supreme Court.

On March 4, 1970, with spring training underway and Flood sitting out the dance, Judge Irving Ben Cooper of the U.S. District Court for the Southern District of New York denied Flood's motion for an injunction. While recognizing the merits of the case, Judge Cooper felt that such a precedent-making decision should be made by the nation's highest court. Flood went into exile in Denmark while Goldberg waited for the case to come before the justices.

The long judicial process came to an end with the Supreme Court declining to rule on the legality of the reserve system. The machinery existed, the justices wrote, for the system to be altered through negotiations between the Players Association and owners. It was crushing news for Flood, who attempted a brief comeback with the dismal Washington Senators before the Supreme Court non-decision. He had squandered nearly two years of his career. A bitter, confused man, Flood spent half a decade running a tourist bar on the island of Majorca, where the only baseball news he ever heard was relayed by sailors on leave from the U.S. Sixth Fleet.

Marvin Miller was wrong about one thing. Flood found a job in baseball. In one of life's small ironies, he was hired for the 1978 season to be a color man and analyst. The man who hired him as a member of the Oakland A's broadcast crew was none other than Charles O. Finley.

Flood had sown the seeds of rebellion. It remained for others to reap the harvest.

In the winter of 1975, a Los Angeles righthander named Andy Messersmith and a Montreal lefthander named Dave McNally brought the reserve clause crashing down.

The machinery for change was oiled during 1972 negotiations between the players and owners,

a deadlocked attempt to hammer out a new basic agreement which resulted in a 10-day strike, the first concerted job action in major league history. Part of the agreement that ended the strike was a binding arbitration process to resolve salary and contract disputes. Fittingly, Finley was in the eye of the first arbitration hurricane.

Jim ("Catfish") Hunter was the American League's premier righthander, a perennial 20-game winner for the A's. Hunter sought his free agency on grounds that Finley reneged on an interest-free $150,000 loan that was part of his contract. Finley could have easily settled the matter out of court.

Charles O. Finley, who brought baseball its DH rule, midweek playoff and World Series games, and multicolored, double-knit uniforms, showed there is room for change.

But the man often seemed to have a death wish when it came to fights he couldn't hope to win.

Peter J. Seitz, a federal arbitrator, ruled that Finley had breached his contract with Hunter. The pitcher was a free agent, Seitz said, and he could sign with any major league team, including the A's, if he so chose. Hunter sat back and watched the offers roll in. As the doomsayers predicted, a wild bidding war ensued and Hunter signed a $2.8 million contract with the Yankees. Meanwhile, the reserve clause remained intact until Seitz unleashed another thunderbolt.

The cornerstone of the reserve system was the right of a club to automatically renew an unsigned player's contract for a period of one year. The player's only safeguard was that his salary could not be cut by more than 20 percent in any automatic renewal. Neither McNally nor Messersmith signed 1975 contracts. Their clubs dutifully applied the automatic renewal provision.

Both pitchers submitted their cases to arbitration, claiming the clubs had no right to extend their contracts.

On December 24, 1975, Seitz sent baseball a message. It was not, "Merry Christmas." The arbitrator became the Grinch who stole the reserve clause. He ruled that by virtue of their having failed to sign 1975 contracts, the automatic renewal clauses had lapsed. Messersmith and McNally were free agents. The reserve clause was nothing more than a one-year option.

There was a wailing and gnashing of teeth from sea to shining sea. Dick Young, a syndicated columnist for the New York *Daily News,* had bitterly opposed the trend toward free agency. His column on Seitz's historic ruling was an accurate barometer of the Establishment mood.

"Peter Seitz reminds me of a terrorist," Young wrote, "a little man to whom nothing very important has happened in his lifetime, who suddenly decides to create some excitement by tossing a bomb into things. What Peter Seitz has ruled, in effect, is that there is no reserve clause. He has made it possible for a ballplayer to walk away from his team in one year. To trade himself, in actuality. Peter Seitz, labor arbitrator, has decided to overrule the Supreme Court of the United States. This is pretty much like a traffic court judge deciding that Standard Oil is in violation of the antitrust laws. . . ."

If you get the idea the Establishment was upset, you're right.

There was no stampede toward overt free agency, though. Even militants in the Players As-sociation agreed that there was a need for a modified reserve system. But the owners, acting more on blind faith and wretched legal advice than in a spirit of compromise, fought to have the Seitz ruling overturned. They went into court like a single kamikaze diving toward an aircraft carrier. Once more, they went down in flames.

A district court judge upheld the Seitz ruling. The hawks wanted to take it to the Supreme Court, but their best legal minds told them that they would lose this time around.

It was 1976 and the basic agreement was up for renewal once again. The owners padlocked the spring training camps until Commissioner Kuhn poked another sharp stick in their eye. Kuhn ordered the camps opened and told the players and owners to proceed with the season while continuing to negotiate. In August, both sides agreed to a temporary, experimental, drastically-modified reserve system. A player with six years major league service could become a free agent after playing one "option" year without a contract. He would then be eligible for a reentry draft in which up to 12 teams could acquire the right to sign him. The team which originally owned his contract was also eligible to retain negotiating rights. In 1979, the 44 players who filed for the re-entry draft signed contracts totaling $23 million, most of them complex, multi-year agreements containing performance clauses, no-trade covenants and guaranteed payment.

The same owners who wailed that free agency would bring the game's swift demise couldn't wait to take part in the auction. By the 1981 season, the Yankees, owned by shipping magnate George Steinbrenner, had awarded more than $30 million in free agent contracts.

But the free agent stampede created unprecedented interest in baseball. The publicity generated by free agent negotiations gave the game a second season. By the end of the 1980 season, two players, strikeout artist Nolan Ryan of Houston and .390 hitter George Brett of Kansas City, were earning salaries of $1 million a year.

In that awesome salary context, it is amusing to remember the words of Babe Ruth after he signed a record $80,000 contract for the 1930 season.

"Babe," a sportswriter prodded, "do you realize you make more money now than President Hoover?"

"Why not?" The Babe snapped. "I had a better year."

17

2

2

Bread and Circuses

Here he comes, sliding down from the top of the upper deck like a ruptured peacock, this screwball wearing water skis, for crying out loud. Wearing stubby water skis and dangling from a trapeze bar attached to the kind of kite they tow behind speedboats above the placid waters of Cypress Gardens.

But this is no milk run behind a boat headed into the steady winds of central Florida. Kiteman I is starting a journey into the unknown and the press box cynics are laying 5–1 that the guy will make the obituary columns.

Here he comes and now the smoke bombs attached to the wings of the kite—a hang glider, actually—are belching lavender smoke. It is opening night in Veterans Stadium, the 65,000-seat facility which in 1971 replaced falling-down Connie Mack Stadium, an obsolete ballyard in the middle of the North Philadelphia ghetto. Kiteman I is halfway down the ramp now. The plan is for him to swoop into majestic flight from the first row of the upper deck and ride the wind currents some 500 feet to home plate, where he will hand the first ball to catcher Tim McCarver. But Kiteman I twists off the ramp halfway through his descent and cartwheels into a section of empty seats like a winged partridge. "Oh, well," Phillies vice-president Bill Giles says, "better to fail your Wasserman test than never to love at all."

What's that X-rated chicken doing now? Oh, he's making lascivious advances toward the buxom beauty in a halter top behind the San Diego dugout. What else is new? Now he's back out on the field, where he sneaks up behind plate umpire Bruce Froemming and makes precisely the same motion with his right leg that dogs make when they find a lamppost or fire plug which meets their needs. This chicken, Ted Giannoulas, the San Diego Chicken, would make Colonel Sanders turn over in his grave.

Three time zones to the east, David Raymond, imaginative son of the University of Delaware football coach Tubby Raymond, is doing his thing, surrounded by the fanciful trappings of a jolly, bumbling, green aardvark. While the San Diego

Chicken keys his humor to adults, the Phillie Phanatic never does anything you wouldn't let the kids watch on Sesame Street. *In fact, the same folks who gave America's preschoolers Big Bird and the Cookie Monster designed Raymond's costume. There's a lot of athleticism involved in Giannoulas' routines and he designed his chicken suit with an eye for headfirst slides into bases, somersaults into the stands after imaginary foul balls, and reckless runs at fair damsels. Raymond's costume is so cumbersome he is forced to make up for his inability to navigate crisply with superb mimicry and slapstick gyrations worthy of Laurel and Hardy.*

But what do our feathered friends have to do with baseball? Is it America's most sophisticated game or an aviary?

Purists blanch at the proliferation of team mascots and other gimmickry that clutters the ballpark landscape as baseball careens into the eighties. They prefer their baseball neat. But purists are a fast-fading minority.

They long for the days when life was simpler, when you sat in the sun-washed bleachers for 50 cents and watched men dressed in basic white and gray play the game of your youth in God's own sunshine on His green grass. They long for the simple pleasure of coming to the park early, the anticipation building deliciously as the teams go through the timeless ritual of batting and infield practice, still as stylized and traditional as they were at the turn of the century.

Now it is 20 minutes to game time, the starting pitchers are warming up on the sidelines and the ground crew works the infield into pristine smoothness, chalks afresh the batter's box, the coaching boxes behind first and third base and the infield foul lines, reaffirming the game's unique geometry.

In Chicago's rococo Wrigley Field, the National League's last monument to a gentler time, the venerable Pat Piper announced the starting lineups for more than 50 years. During preelectronic days, Piper stood at home plate with a megaphone, never varying the timeless announcement:

Preceding pages: Some strange birds are appearing in baseball, including this one at Baltimore. Opposite top: Chicago's Wrigley Field, where baseball is a day game. Opposite bottom: Candlestick Park, San Francisco.

"Tenshun! Ladies and gentlemen, boys and girls, have your pencils and scorecards ready. Here are today's starting lineups . . ."

The purists tend to forget, however, that for the first 40 years of the century, baseball was the only important professional game in town. It reigned supreme with no real rival for national attention, save for college football, a game that intruded on baseball's space on only a few Saturdays in late September and early October. The National Football League was a struggling infant which rarely filled stadiums. Basketball was a winter diversion which had little spectator impact until promoters began to display it in large arenas like Madison Square Garden and Chicago Stadium. Few could foresee a day when at least 20 colleges would construct indoor palaces seating more than 15,000 fans, or that a 24-team professional league would play from mid-September until mid-June.

Professional hockey, an import from Canada stocked largely by Canadians, was played at the major league level only in New York, Boston, Chicago, and Detroit. It was, however, the best organized of baseball's distant rivals, the national sport in Montreal and Toronto, and staunchly supported by fans in the National Hockey League's four U.S. franchises.

Radio broadcasts, which began to proliferate in the thirties, were a great promotion for major league baseball, despite predictions that they would drag down attendance. "Why should I give my product away for nothing?" more than one owner thundered, a sentiment which turned to grudging approval as well-heeled sponsors jumped on baseball's bandwagon.

Even at the depths of the Depression, baseball prospered. Americans tended to reserve what little surplus cash they could scrape together for family entertainment. More important, with no competition to distract its loyal clientele, baseball had absolutely no reason to promote itself. The newspapers did that job for them nicely, providing daily free advertising from the first day of spring training to the last out of the season. Club payrolls were incredibly small. In the thirties, the average club's total salaries for 28 players rarely topped $150,000. Teams strapped for working capital—the Philadelphia Athletics were a notorious example—regularly sold their top players to wealthier teams. Connie Mack stayed in business more than 50 years by assembling championship teams, underpaying the players, and, finally, selling them in their career primes, beginning the cycle anew by purchasing

*Although the game has an ageless and essentially con-
servative nature, changes do occur. This All Star
game will be played indoors on artificial turf. The
scoreboard presents Old Glory in electronic splendor.*

23

young players at bargain rates from the independent minor leagues of that era.

So, as baseball moved into the postwar prosperity of the fifties there was no reason to give fans more than a five-cent scorecard and the game itself. There were 16 teams in two leagues, travel was by train, and major league baseball did not exist west of St. Louis.

Television, the invention which, more than all other socioeconomic factors combined, caused a tremendous explosion in all areas of spectator sport, came toddling out of the experimental laboratories.

On May 17, 1939, a baseball game between Columbia University and NYU was telecast. The first TV play-by-play man was famed radio sportscaster Bill Stern. Reception was wretched on the handful of crude receivers in existence in the New York area.

On August 26, 1939, five days before Hitler's panzers rolled into Poland, an event which guaranteed that commercial television would stay on the back burner until 1945, a doubleheader between the Dodgers and Reds was telecast.

Those early attempts seemed to prove one thing: Baseball did not lend itself to the new medium. The ball was too difficult to follow. The cameras of the day were suited only for certain types of entertainment. Boxing and wrestling, with the action compressed within a relatively small area, offered bright possibilities, particularly because the lighting could be controlled. Joining early TV stars like Dave Garroway, Ed Sullivan, Milton Berle, and Edward R. Murrow were guys named Gorgeous George and Chief Don Eagle, Jersey Joe Walcott, and Ralph Tiger Jones. Boxing became such a staple on the tube that small clubs which depended on a live audience for existence withered and died. And their demise led to an eventual decline in talent that almost killed the manly art. When ratings followed suit, the Monday night, Wednesday night, Friday night, and Saturday night fights faded into history. Boxing didn't make a comeback as serious TV fare until a bombastic young black heavyweight named Cassius Clay, who used techniques he learned while watching TV wrestlers promote themselves, dragged boxing off the scrap heap.

Television and football were made for each other. Although played over a surface of more than 45,000 square feet, football's singular violence was compressed into an area usually no more than 15 yards wide. As the state of the art was raised, different lenses were developed to highlight or isolate various phases of the action. Through judicious positioning and use of close-up, telephoto, and wide-angle cameras, it became possible for an enlightened producer and director to piece together a coherent and compelling visual account of the crunching action.

Baseball had no such luck. Telephoto shots gave viewers a look only at the pitcher, hitter, and catcher. Wide shots reduced players to the size of ants and the ball was impossible to follow once it bounded through or rocketed over the infield.

By 1958, some telecasts of major sporting events were in color and the nationally televised NFL title game between the New York Giants and Baltimore Colts was a landmark. As a live spectator event it was memorable to those lucky enough to have tickets. As a TV event, though, it was pure theater. The Colts provided the competitive drama, winning the title in the first overtime in NFL history. But the superb camera work raised the bitterly contested, see-saw contest to the level of fine art. Pro football, rising steadily in popularity for 20 years, suddenly exploded. For six hours on Sundays in the autumn and early winter, football became the opiate of the masses.

"Never look back," Satchel Paige once said, "somethin' might be gaining." Suddenly, baseball's monopoly was threatened by an old but never feared rival, a sport which had learned to use the exciting new medium wisely and well.

Suddenly, Bill Veeck didn't look like such a buffoon.

Veeck had long been a neon sign among owners who believed the best form of advertising was no advertising at all, an outgoing maverick who had a fireworks-spouting scoreboard when his colleagues figured a high-powered promotion was inviting a local high school band to play the national anthem on opening day. On August 18, 1951, Veeck outraged decent baseball men everywhere and delighted the rest of the country by sending a 43-inch midget, Eddie Gaedel, up to pinch-hit for the last place St. Louis Browns. Anticipating the furor, Veeck had signed Gaedel to a legal contract and the midget walked on four pitches. The stunt didn't lift the Browns out of the cellar, but attendance picked up and Veeck was across the top of the sports pages for days.

"Veeck's madcap antics have never before violated good taste," *New York Times* columnist Arthur Daly wrote, "but this one is positively indecent, an ignoble burlesque of a noble sport. . . ."

Something old, something new. Top: *Boston's classic scoreboard in Fenway Park where each number is put in place by hand.* Bottom: *Boston's lineup, presented electronically on an opponent's sophisticated display.*

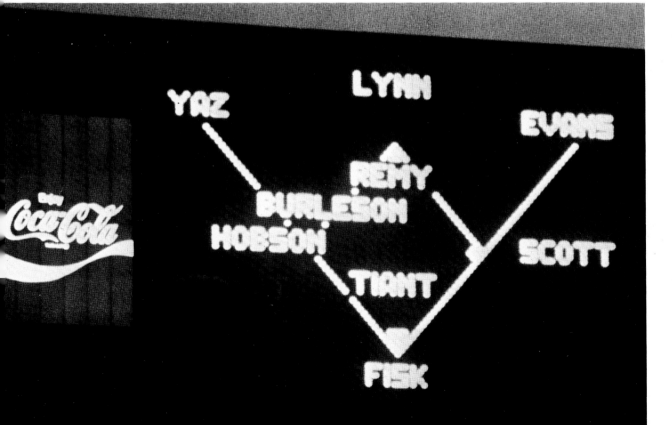

Among Veeck's many ignoble burlesques, his "Fan Participation Night" was the best. Several weeks after the Gaedel caper, Veeck let fans seated in a special section select the starting lineup and make all major tactical decisions by holding up cards that said "Yes" or "No." It was terrific fun and the Browns beat the A's 4–3.

Charles O. Finley was another maverick who refused to believe that the game's mildewed traditions had been handed down from on high along with the Dead Sea Scrolls. In an effort to bolster the A's sagging attendance in Kansas City, Finley had sheep grazing behind the outfield fences and a mechanical rabbit that popped from the ground next to home plate whenever the umpire needed a fresh supply of baseballs. Needless to say, neither concept caught on.

It remained for William Yale Giles to give the promotional side of baseball its shape and substance for the 1980s.

Giles was no gyspy moving from franchise to franchise with a bag of tricks. The Denison University graduate was a baseball blueblood. His father, Hall of Fame executive Warren Giles, was a former president of the Cincinnati Reds who later served a long and distinguished term as president of the National League. In fact, he was a man who spent most of his life close to the tip of baseball's Establishment iceberg.

"My first brush with promotions came in high school," Bill Giles says. "I was president of our fraternity my senior year. We always held our annual dance at the least expensive place we could find and hired a kids band for next to nothing. I decided we would do something very big, sell fifteen hundred tickets, and hire a name big band. I rented the biggest hall in Cincinnati and instead of paying a hundred fifty dollars for a band we paid twelve hundred. It worked. I don't know if we made a lot of money, but we made a profit."

Bill Giles went to college and served in the Air Force. After his discharge, he decided that what he wanted to do in a life rich with possibilities was work in the front office phase of baseball. He started at the bottom, working as part-time business manager of the Reds' Nashville farm team in the South Atlantic League. That's where Giles began his calculated craziness, a flair for the promotional unusual which he would cultivate with the Houston Colt .45s and Astros and hone into the state of the art with the Phillies.

When the National League expanded to 10 teams in 1962, Giles, then 24, went to Houston with Reds executive Gabe Paul as a front office assistant with undefined duties.

"I went down there and got involved with Judge Roy Hofheinz, who became the majority owner of the club," Giles says. "We got involved in building the organization from the ground up. After about four months, Judge Hofheinz got into a big argument with Gabe Paul.

"Gabe wanted to enlarge the Houston minor league park to about thirty thousand seats and play there for two years until the Domed Stadium was ready. The judge wanted to spend about two million dollars and build a temporary park near the construction site of the Dome. His reasoning was that he wanted people to get into the habit of driving to a part of the city where the Dome would be. Paul thought it was ridiculous to spend that much money for a throwaway ballpark."

Hofheinz won. Ramshackle Colt .45 Stadium was thrown together a tumbleweed-roll from the acreage where baseball's most remarkable facility was rising.

Judge Hofheinz was not a baseball man, but he was a shaker and mover who knew how to get things done. The Harris County Domed Stadium was his brainchild, the building which finally bankrupted the old man and sent the Astros as they were later called into receivership. Hofheinz lived his final years as a semi-invalid in a wheelchair, but his contribution to the modern game of baseball was as revolutionary in its way as was that of Charles O. Finley, and he left a powerful imprint on the promotional philosophies of Bill Giles.

Thanks to an unforeseen accident of nature, six teams now play their games on artificial surfaces. When the Astrodome opened in 1965, the playing surface was sodded with a special strain of grass developed by the University of Houston which would subsist on a minimal amount of ultraviolet light.

"It worked," Giles remembers, "but it was brittle as hell. It just couldn't stand up to the pounding it took in baseball. That wasn't our only problem in the Dome.

"For the grass to grow properly, the Dome roof panels had to admit light. The glare was so bad that fielders had a terrible time seeing fly balls. It was a joke watching big league ballplayers cringing out there to keep from getting hit in the head. So we semiopaqued about three-quarters of the panels and blacked out a section that was the background for most fly balls. The players could see the ball better, but the grass died. Grady Hatton, our man-

Philadelphia's team mascot, the Phillie Phanatic, is one of several unique creatures used by teams to promote attendance and entertain the fans. The Phanatic costume was created by Jim Hensen's Muppet makers.

ager, wanted to make it an all-dirt field like some he had seen in Japan, but that didn't get much of a response. Nobody could picture playing in a spectacular place like the Astrodome and having a dirt floor."

Judge Hofheinz rode to the rescue. He had heard that the Monsanto Corporation, the giant chemical conglomerate, had developed an artificial grass for use as a patio covering and outdoor carpeting.

"The judge contacted the Monsanto people and told them the problem," Giles says. "They sent some experts out and said they could carpet the entire playing surface. Hofheinz asked what it would cost and they told him one million dollars. The judge was really fast on his feet. He said that if Monsanto made the installation for nothing he would let them call it AstroTurf. Monsanto immediately saw the commercial possibilities and agreed to lay down the vast plastic rug for nothing." As treated in the next chapter, artificial surfaces have created the need for athletes fleet enough of foot to deal with the increased velocity imparted to the baseball by the surface's low rolling resistance. As lefthanded pitcher Jim Kaat said after his first start on AstroTurf, "It's like shooting marbles in a bathtub."

AstroTurf helped propel Giles into the national sports headlines, thanks to a running feud with feisty Chicago Cubs manager Leo Durocher, who hated everything about the Astrodome from the ballpark's distant fences to the plastic blades which once prompted slugger Dick Allen to remark, "I don't like to play on nothing a horse can't graze on."

Among his varied duties in the early days of the Dome, Giles operated—orchestrated would say it better—baseball's first computerized message board and scoreboard, a marvel of animation and editorial capability that has been widely copied. Everything about the scoreboard infuriated Durocher.

"They got these giant bleeping hands up there that tell the fans when to clap, for chrissakes," Leo would fume. "Where I come from the fans don't need to be told when to clap."

Durocher also discovered to his vast chagrin that the message board also had the capacity to insult, and Giles, sensing he had a live one on the hook, programmed a series of one-liners and innuendos designed to drive Durocher up the wall.

"The first time he saw the Dome, Durocher said it was a place where players should be wearing tennis sneakers. That Christmas I took a piece of the old sod we had replaced with AstroTurf, put it in a box with an old pair of tennis sneakers, and sent it to Leo as a present. I got a little static over that."

His flair for scoreboard literature almost resulted in Giles's banishment from baseball. Umpire John Kibler went on a spree where he ejected Astro

players from four consecutive games. Giles decided to have some fun.

"After the fourth ejection of one of our players, I put up on the message board, 'Kibler's Done It Again,'" Giles recalls. "The fans started to really get all over him. The next morning my father, who was league president at the time, called me and said, 'Bill, who was responsible for the thing on the scoreboard about the umpire?' I said, 'Gee, Dad, I'm not sure who it is, but I'll tell him to never do it again.' He said, 'Well, when you find out who it was tell him his allowance has been cut off.'"

Bill's next exercise of his First Amendment rights put him on the carpet of Commissioner Bowie Kuhn. There had been a major 1969 trade which sent outfielder Rusty Staub to Montreal for first baseman Donn Clendenon. Clendenon refused to report to the Astros and Houston screamed for Staub's return. Instead of voiding the deal, Kuhn awarded the Astros pitchers John Billingham, Skip Guinn, and an unspecified amount of cash. Giles, eager to ride the fans' sense of outrage, flashed a multiple-choice quiz on the message board:

"Who is the most unpopular person in Houston?

(a) Pete Rozelle
(b) Frankenstein
(c) Xxxxx Xxxx"

"Naturally, the fans figured out who the X's represented and they roared when I flashed the answer," he says. "The wire services picked it up and the next day I was on a plane to New York. Kuhn was angry. He told me I was degrading the office of the commissioner and that if I ever did it again he would kick me out of baseball."

Bill Giles was ready for the Big-Time promotional circuit.

The Phillies were down on their luck as they prepared to move from ramshackle Connie Mack Stadium to 65,000-seat Veterans Stadium for the 1971 season. In 1970, only the presence of the expansion Montreal Expos kept them from finishing in the Eastern Division cellar in the first year of divisional play. They were a sorry 73–88 and drew only 708,247 fans. The highlights of the season came after the final game played in the old ballpark, when the crowd took the stands apart like a plague of locusts, ripping out whole rows of seats, walking into the North Philadelphia night carrying urinals and beating one another upside the head with seat slats which had been handed out as ill-advised souvenirs.

Owner Bob Carpenter was from the old

school. He filled his front office with cronies and prized loyalty and willingness to work for small wages above performance. But the heir to the Carpenter half of the DuPont fortune (probably valued in excess of $100 million today) could feel the hot winds of change. He knew it would take more than a dozen old pals to run what would become the league's biggest park. The front office staff would have to be upgraded and greatly increased in number. Carpenter had heard good things about how young Bill Giles, Warren's son, was putting people into the Astrodome to watch a team even shabbier than the Phillies.

Bill was brought in as vice-president of business operations after the 1969 season and made little effort to launch his flying circus in Connie Mack Stadium, directing his energies into the move to the Vet.

Bob Carpenter was a hard sell. He was from a school of baseball operation which traditionally held that the only promotion necessary was to hang out a "Gates Open" sign, play a scratchy recording of the national anthem, and get on with the ball game. The problem was, the Phillies were a wretched team years from contention even with the most inspired rebuilding program. And in 1970, people were finding other things to do with their entertainment dollar. Venturing into the mean North Philadelphia ghetto was an unsettling experience. A great market area of more than six million potential fans living within an hour of the ballpark had fallen into decay. Giles knew he would be busy.

"I'd throw some ideas at Bob and he'd say, 'Jesus, why do you want to do that?' I'd say, 'Bob, just leave me alone.' I told him fans had gotten out of the habit of coming out to our baseball games. That as recently as 1964, we had drawn one point six million fans, so there must have been interest. I felt we were still getting the hard-core fan. What we had to do was get the fan with semi-interest back to the ballpark and make it a good place to come, so he'd have fun and come back again. We had to attract more young fans, who would become our attendance base in seasons to come."

In 1971, Giles filled the sparkling new stadium with a barrage of promotions, circus acts, musical entertainments, merchandise giveaways, and reduced-price ticket plans. Attendance jumped to 1.5 million, but Giles knew that in a few seasons, higher salaries, inflation, and soaring minor league expenditures would drive his break-even point to 2 million fans and above. He had to maintain a blitz of sideshows unprecedented in baseball history. The novelty of visiting a new stadium, which attracted many fans in 1971, would soon wear off.

He decided early on that he would start each season with unorthodox ways of delivering the traditional first pitch to home plate, preferably from the air—very high in the air. For the inaugural Vet opener, the first ball was dropped from a helicopter hovering some 300 feet above the plate to catcher Mike Ryan, who managed to catch it with a desperate lunge.

The strike-delayed 1972 opener brings us to the delicious saga of Kiteman I, the closest Giles has come to doing what many insist he will do someday: Kill his opening day act.

"I was sitting around in the off-season wracking my brain for an opening day first-ball act," Giles says. "I was looking through a *Sports Illustrated* and came across a piece about a guy in California who jumped off cliffs harnessed to a kite—one of the pioneer hang-gliders. I called the magazine and they gave me the guy's number. He agreed to try it, but then we lost the first week of the season to the strike and opening day was set back. The guy called me and said he had to go to Mexico for three weeks to teach the president of Mexico to water ski with a kite."

Giles, who had heavily advertised the spectacular sight of a man flying a ball from the upper deck in centerfield to home plate suspended from a kite, was in a state of panic. He went to the Yellow Pages and located a ski-boat dealer in the suburbs who said a friend of his from the water circus in Cypress Gardens, Florida, might be interested.

"He agreed to come up and look at what I had in mind and he told me there was no way he'd try it. But he said if I got him out in the parking lot on roller skates and towed him behind a car he might be able to get up about four hundred feet and fly into the stadium. I ran that by Mayor Rizzo and he turned thumbs down—too many traffic problems, safety problems, things like that. So I offered the guy another five hundred dollars and he agreed to try it—reluctantly. I said I wanted him to make a practice run. He said, 'No way. If I'm gonna kill myself doing this crazy thing I want more people watching me than you and a couple of office secretaries.' He said the only way he could get properly launched was for us to build him a ramp he could slide down to pick up the speed he needed to keep from dropping into the lower deck. The damn ramp cost me more money than Kiteman I."

The great feat was attempted on a gelid April night of swirling wind. Kiteman I stood at the top of the takeoff ramp paralyzed by growing fear.

"After he was introduced, he was supposed to light the smoke bombs on his wing tips and take off after the organist gave him a big fanfare. He lit the smoke bombs, the organ played a few flourishes and . . ."

Nothing. After watching Kiteman, frozen there like a parakeet trapped by a stalking cat, the 45,000 fans began to boo. And boo.

Giles picked up his walkie-talkie and asked an aide standing with the aerialist to explain the delay. Paul Callahan put it simply, "He says he's scared to death."

"I hollered, 'Go ahead, jump; the fans are getting impatient,'" Callahan remembers. "He gave me a terrified look and said, 'What the hell,' and went wobbling down the ramp."

And into aviation history, taking his place alongside the Wright Brothers, Wrong Way Corrigan, and the Hindenburg, Kiteman I careened off the ramp and crashed into the upper deck seats like a winged mallard. "I thought he was dead," Giles says. "It was the low point of my career. The fans are booing like crazy and there's my great act in a crumpled heap after a thirty-foot flight. But then he came up waving and made a helluva throw to the plate and I felt a little better."

Since then, Kiteman II has made it halfway to second base and Kiteman III, using superior glider technology, and a running start down a more gradually sloping ramp, actually fluttered the 500 feet to home plate amid a thundering ovation.

Other opening day Giles aerial extravaganzas include a first-ball delivery by a sky diver, a guy shot out of a cannon from the mound to home plate, and an appearance by the Golden Knights, the crack Army exhibition parachute team which landed with precison at first, second, third, the mound, and home plate.

So far, nobody has been killed, but Giles and the Vet are still young and if you know of anybody with an aerial schtick and a strong death wish, Bill Giles would be glad to hear from him.

In more terrestrial activities, Giles figures he's given away enough bats in a decade to denude a good-sized forest, and enough helmets, batting gloves, jackets, tote bags, and T-shirts to keep a South Korean village fully employed working 12-hour shifts. Musical attractions include concerts by Dionne Warwick, Seals and Crofts, Pat Benatar, and Ronnie Milsap. Is it all worth it?

Well, the Phillies have topped 2.4 million fans for six straight seasons.

3

Game in Motion

According to apocryphal legend, Sir Isaac Newton was lazing under a tree contemplating the wonders of nature when an apple zapped him on the noggin. "By Jove," Newton exclaimed. "I believe that's, uh, gravity."

A couple of centuries later, a swinging statesman-inventor in King George's Colonies, was flying a kite in a thunderstorm. The ribald humor of the times has it that Ben Franklin was trying to fly his room key to Dolly Madison and found it a shocking experience. Enter electricity.

Unfortunately, history has obscured the identity of the genius who sometime in the 1840s or so decided that the distance between the bases in an infant game featuring a bat and ball should be 90 feet. Was it Alexander Cartwright? Abner Doubleday? Nobody seems to know for sure. Baseball's embryo evolution remains hazy. But the man who decided that the distance between bases should be 90 feet insured that baseball would be popular forever. It is a distance which blessed the game with almost perfect geometry, a delicate balance between the time it takes a player to run 90 feet and the time required for a fielder to catch a ground ball and throw it to first base. It guaranteed that a vast majority of balls hit on the ground to the infielders would end in close decisions at first base and that time frame holds true for almost every baseball play that involves a player running and a fielder trying to throw him out—the ball hit into the outfield corners, which results in a close play at second or third, the ball hit deep between outfielders, which requires a relay throw from outfielder to infielder, and the stolen base. Ninety feet! Yes. Sheer genius? Or happy accident?

The runner edges a few feet off first base, then jumps out to a brazen lead. The second baseman cups his glove and hollers to the shortstop. The hitter is righthanded, so he'll cover second base. The righthanded pitcher peers owlishly to see the catcher's sign, then looks nervously over his left shoulder. He throws lazily to first base, just to let the runner know he's out there. The stadium organist

pierces the night with a cavalry charge. The fans respond. Once more, the long-legged black man on first base jumps out to that brazen lead, both feet securely planted on the artificial grass beyond the dirt cutout. This time the pitcher unfurls his best move and the runner is forced to scramble back to first with a dusty, head-first slide.

The runner has this pitcher measured. He's seen his casual move and his money move. He could care less about the catcher. If the runner does his job right, if he knows that once the pitcher's left leg starts toward the plate it will take him 1.5 seconds to release the pitch and another .5 seconds for the ball to travel the 60 feet 6 inches to the plate, he's got it made, because there's no way even the best-throwing catcher who ever lived can set up to make the long throw to second base in the 1.3 seconds it will take to defeat his 3.3 speed.

As the pitcher goes into his stretch the third time, the runner takes an even bigger lead. Through close study, he knows this particular pitcher doesn't like to make two hard throws to first in a row. This time, he'll either lob the ball to first again—in which case the runner can loaf back to the bag—or he'll finally go to the plate. The pitcher's kick leg poises for a millisecond, then starts in the direction of the plate. The runner explodes off his back leg. By his second stride he is at full speed. The catcher's throw is low and late. It skids into center field.

Using a bounce-up slide that enables him to be at full speed once again and making a turn for third, the runner easily takes the extra base while the centerfielder retrieves the ball.

For the swift runner with the offensive ability to reach base a high percentage of the time, modern baseball is like shooting fish in a barrel. All the physical improvements which have come to baseball have helped make his swift art easier to employ. The artificial surfaces have given him a bouncy, lightning-fast track to run on. Footwear is lighter and more efficient than the heavy leather and metal spikes his forefathers wore to run on grass and lumpy clay. His form-fitting uniform pro-

32

motes a full range of body motion and presents less resistance to the wind his swift running creates.

The most dramatic change in professional baseball during the last decade, one which will continue unabated during the eighties, is the reemergence of the speed game, featuring the stolen base and players with the running ability to leg singles into doubles and doubles into triples. It was a natural reaction by the offense to a game which was slowly being dominated by pitchers, men who all seemed to tower 6 feet 4 inches and who could depend on help from a bullpen specialist with gunfighter eyes and a nasty "trick" pitch like a fork ball, or on a fastball that rushed up to the plate trailing blue sparks.

In the 38 years between 1930 and 1968, major league baseball went full cycle, from a game of robust offense to a game almost totally dominated by pitchers. Consider that in 1930, one team, the Philadelphia Phillies, had a team average of .315. A team average! Five regulars hit over .300. Despite all this offense, the Phillies finished in last place with 102 losses.

In 1930, the ball had so much rabbit in it you could hear a heartbeat and major league pitching was dreadful. No fewer than nine teams hit more than .300 as units. The entire National League average was .303. Stumpy Cubs outfielder Hack Wilson sobered up long enough to slam 56 homers and drive in 190 runs—baseball's most unassailable record. There were so many .300 hitters in both leagues that the Top 10 carried by newspapers was cutting off at about the .350 level. Guys who hit only .325 in 1930 were asked to take salary cuts.

Take 1968—take it, please, most hitters were saying. Only five National League hitters finished over .300. Legends like Willie Mays (.289), Henry Aaron (.287), and Roberto Clemente (.291) wondered if they had gone to sleep only to wake up playing a different game on a strange planet.

In 810 games played in the National League, there were 185 shutouts pitched. Bob Gibson, the towering, scowling ace of the St. Louis Cardinals, finished the season with an earned run average of 1.12, a mark which was not matched even by the stars of the floppy-glove, dead-ball era, when the spitball and other bizarre pitches were legal and the average hitter was about the size of Mickey Rooney.

Opposite: A Met runner sprints the 90 feet from home to first, a magical distance that always seems to produce a close play. Above: *A play at the plate. Speed on the base paths has offset the edge of modern pitchers.*

Teams started running in self-defense. You couldn't win if you couldn't score and you couldn't score if you never got runners past second base. Alarmed by the dearth of runs and a corresponding sag in attendance, the Lords of Baseball lowered the mound and put a little more juice in the ball. But even though run production has increased somewhat, and home runs are still being hit in significant numbers, the name of today's game is pitching and speed.

In 1939, Stan Hack led the National League with 17 stolen bases. No base-stealer in the lone-ball era topped 30 until Pete Reiser stole 34 for the 1946 Dodgers. Willie Mays reminded old-timers of the good old days of Ty Cobb, Max Carey, and Bob Bescher when he stole 40 bases for the 1956 Giants. But the stolen base was still spurned by most teams. The home run and the big inning were the preferred ways to put runs on the scoreboard. Why risk a rally-stopping out, when one swing could get you a bundle of runs?

Enter a slim, fragile-looking shortstop named Maurice Morning Wills.

When the Dodgers made their celebrated cross-country move to Los Angeles, Wills was a prisoner in the club's far-flung farm system, waiting for Pee Wee Reese, one of the aging Boys of Summer, to retire.

Maury was 28 when he finally became the regular Dodgers shortstop in 1960. Nothing in his long minor league background suggested that he would someday be the man to break Cobb's single-season stolen base record, that in 1962 he would become the first man in baseball history to steal 100 bases (104) and set in motion a conservative, play-for-one-run style. But Wills was a man for his time and his team.

The move to Los Angeles left the aging Dodger juggernaut playing in 95,000-seat Los Angeles Coliseum while their new stadium was being hacked into the Chavez Ravine hillside. The Dodgers found themselves between dynasties, rebuilding from a minor league system which was no longer stocked with power-hitters in the Duke Snider, Gil Hodges, Roy Campanella, Carl Furillo mold. The new stars lived by their legs and their arms. Manager Walter Alston bent to the personnel at hand. Led by Wills, the new Dodgers beat you with a scratch hit, a stolen base, an infield out, and a sacrifice fly. Alston would sit back and hope the opposition didn't score a run off super pitchers like Sandy Koufax and Don Drysdale.

It was a sit-on-the-edge-of-your-seat, nail-biting, nerve-wracking style of baseball but the normally laid-back Southern California fans loved it. They brought bugles to the park and roared whenever Wills or even swifter outfielder Willie Davis got on base. What they didn't know was that Alston was merely buying time until the minor league system and judicious trades enabled him to go back to a more orthodox style. The 1978 Dodgers under Tommy Lasorda became the first club in baseball history to have four players in the lineup—Steve Garvey, Ron Cey, Reggie Smith, and Dusty Baker—to each hit 30 or more home runs.

But the speed trend was well established. Wills handed the base-stealing baton to St. Louis outfielder Lou Brock, a man who combined above average speed and intelligence to shatter every existing career and season stolen base record. During nine remarkable years between 1966 and 1974, Brock led the majors in stolen bases eight times. Running on AstroTurf in Busch Memorial Stadium and studying opposing pitchers the way Albert Einstein studied atomic physics, Brock never stole fewer than 52 bases in that span, and in 1974 at the age of 35, the man they called "Sweet Lou" put Wills's record out of sight with an incredible 118 steals.

At 35, Brock's speed was well past its peak. "There's maybe ten players around who would beat me in a foot race," Lou said as he closed in on the record. "I think I've proved that you steal more with technique and knowledge than with sheer speed. People ask me how much speed I have left and I tell them, 'Just enough.' And that's what it takes. A runner has to have just enough speed to make his knowledge of the pitchers pay off."

Brock could tell you more about a pitcher's habits than the pitcher himself. He knew the half dozen or so pitchers in the league with genuinely good kickoff moves, the ones who were willing to concede the stolen base rather than expend a lot of energy throwing to first base, and the ones who were sincerely interested in holding him close, but had moves to first and to the plate that could be timed by hourglass.

He kept detailed charts and records on every pitcher in the National League and he backed them up with visual documentation. Brock often spent his time between at-bats with a motion picture camera, assembling a film record of every pitcher. Once he had a pitcher's various tendencies and flaws wired, Lou was notoriously tight-lipped about his ability to capitalize on them. One sure way to terminate an interview with the outfielder was to ask

36

him to reveal what he knew about the pitchers he was larcenizing. All he would tell writers about his base-stealing style was, "It takes me ten steps and an average of three point three seconds to get from first to second on a stolen base attempt."

Brock refused to be bound by Old School codes which held that you didn't run when your team had a big lead or was far behind. He often outraged pitchers by stealing second and third in the ninth inning with the Cardinals enjoying a safe lead. Just as often, he upset his own teammates by running when the Cardinals were four or five runs behind, a "dumb play," according to an unwritten book the author of which has never been identified.

"Nobody tells hitters to stop hitting home runs when their team has a big lead," Brock would say. "Why should a base-stealer stop running? They get paid to hit homers. I get paid to steal bases."

Unlike Wills and Joe Morgan, another great base-stealer, Brock didn't believe in taking a huge lead. He figured that the guys who tried to buy an extra step were getting worn out diving back to first and getting pounded with swipe tags executed by 225-pound first basemen. He liked to sort of take a short stroll off the bag, looking casual and exploding when the pitcher tipped off his intentions. By the time he reached his thirties, Lou had broken

pitchers' moves down into four general types, so it was possible for him to steal a base on a pitcher after he saw him make just one or two moves.

And like most great base-stealers, Brock held that it was easier to steal third than second, despite the much shorter throw for the catcher.

"You can get a much better jump off second, because the kickoff move to second is an unnatural one for a pitcher and you can get a huge lead," he said.

Brock stole 70 bases in 1973, a figure experts felt was incredible for a man of 34. He would start to slow down, they predicted. Brock says he regarded the predictions as a challenge. He went into the 1974 season determined not only to have his biggest year on the bases but to break Wills's record. If he had announced his goals on opening day, men wearing white coats would have hustled him off the field.

"At thirty-five years old I stole one hundred eighteen bases just to defy the book, because everyone said it couldn't be done. I didn't write the book. Everyone said it was like a ten-year-old horse winning the Kentucky Derby. But it was the challenge of the moment. One can be the exception to the rule. During spring training I would go around and film all the pitchers at sixteen frames a second to

The walking lead, hit-and-run, and sacrifice, combined
with speed-merchant larceny, are all ways of getting
the runner down to second and into scoring position.

37

Top: *Ron LeFlore gave the Montreal Expos speed on the bases.*
Right: *The umpire's job is to see the ball, focus on the
slide, watch for the tag, and make a split-second call.*
Above: *The late Roberto Clemente, who played with intelligence,
grace, and style.*

find out what part of their body moved first.

What Brock discovered when he started breaking down the films was that it took an average of 3.6 seconds for the pitch to reach the catcher, then for the catcher to pivot, step, and throw the ball to second base. Brock figured, correctly it turned out, that the numbers were all on his side. Sure, he guessed wrong sometimes and was kicked off or run down between first and second. Sure, he got terrible jumps and was gunned out easily by a superb technical catcher like Johnny Bench or Bob Boone.

But he ran to the stopwatch and he knew that 99 percent of the times he broke for second he was operating with an approximate leeway of three-tenths of a second, an eternity in the bang-bang world of baseball.

When one scans the stolen base statistics since Jackie Robinson broke the major league color line in 1947, there are inescapable sociological implications. Although blacks and Latins have dominated most offensive phases of baseball for better than three decades, nowhere is that dominance more lopsided than in the stolen base statistics. Since 1947, when Robinson won the title with a modest total of 29, only one white player, Pee Wee Reese in 1952, has led the National League in stolen bases.

In 1980, of the top 12 base-stealers in both leagues, only Dave Collins of the Reds is white. It was an incredible year for the stolen base. Rickey Henderson of the Oakland A's led the majors with 100 steals as manager Billy Martin declared an all-out running war on American League pitchers. Here are some other things that happened on the bases in 1980, the Year of the Burner:

• For the first time in baseball history, three men, Henderson (100), Montreal's Ron LeFlore (97), and Pittsburgh's Omar Moreno (96), stole more than 90 bases in a season.

• LeFlore and teammate Rodney Scott, who stole 63 bases for the Expos, became the greatest one-two running punch in baseball history.

• San Diego became the first National League team to have three players steal 50 or more bases. Gene Richards (61), Ozzie Smith (57), and Jerry Mumphrey (52) matched a feat by American Leaguers Bill North (75), Bert Campaneris (54), and Don Baylor (52) with Oakland in 1976.

• The major league total of 3,291 stolen bases—an average of 127 per team—was the highest since 1911, when the record of 3,403 was established in a deadball era when teams lived by the bunt and stolen base.

"There's no doubt about it," said Phillies general manager Paul Owens, "the biggest trend in baseball over the past ten years is speed, speed, and more speed. The first thing we look for now when we scout young prospects is speed and overall athletic ability. We've got instructors at the minor league level who can teach the mechanics of hitting and fielding. But you can't teach raw speed. A couple of years ago, we sent a couple of scouts to the Bahamas to look at a big high school kid named Will Culmer. He was six feet, four inches, weighed about two hundred fifteen pounds and he held the Bahamas Federation schoolboy record for the hundred yard dash. We signed the kid even though he had only played about a dozen or so games of amateur baseball. We drafted him as an athlete. Will's still raw, but he hit .369 for us in Class A ball in 1980 and we think he's going to be a future star.

"We play on AstroTurf, where the ball gets through the outfield alleys in a hurry. If you don't have outfielders quick enough to run down balls hit in the gaps you'll get doubled and tripled to death. And when you get players who can run that fast it's only natural they're going to steal some bases."

Despite the elevation of the stolen base to a position of respectability unrivaled since the days of George White's "Scandals" and the Ziegfeld Girl, the power game is far from dead. It is just scuffling a little, thanks to the move of many franchises into vast, all-purpose stadiums usually shared with teams from the National Football League. This is particularly true in the National League, where the sole survivor of the bandbox era is Chicago's Wrigley Field, truly an historic shrine and the only major league ball park without lights. It is a sign of the times in the National League that Candlestick Park, dedicated in 1960, is now the Senior Circuit's second oldest park. And the Dodgers and Cubs are the only National League teams which do not share a stadium with a football team.

Just as it lagged far behind the National League in the signing of black players after 1947, the American League has new stadiums in only four cities—Kansas City, Oakland, Anaheim, and Seattle. Texas, Baltimore, Toronto, and Minnesota play in expanded minor league ball parks. Failure to keep pace with the National League in expansion of physical facilities is an important reason why the American League's product has shown slippage in the past 20 years, despite excellent results in World Series competition. The widening gap in attendance, profits, and top to bottom league strength is

a major reason why National League owners are currently opposed to realignment of the leagues along geographical lines and to inter-league play during the regular season.

Most of the new stadiums are symmetrical in their baseball dimensions, which penalizes the power hitter. Jack Murphy Stadium in San Diego and the Astrodome in Houston are among the most difficult home run parks in baseball history.

Wrigley Field remains a shooting gallery for power hitters, particularly when the wind is blowing straight out on a hot summer day. But that aid to the home run hitter is often cancelled when the wind turns around and blows off Lake Michigan into the hitter's face. Of the new National League stadiums, only Fulton County Stadium in Atlanta, which features light air and low outfield fences, is a shooting gallery in the old Crosley Field, Connie Mack Stadium, Ebbets Field tradition.

In the American League, Yankee Stadium is still tailored for the lefthanded pull hitter despite massive renovation. Fenway Park in Boston still features the Green Monster, a pitcher's nightmare of a tall and inconveniently close fence in left field. A combination of a piano-mover lineup and the favorable dimensions of Milwaukee County Stadium have turned the current Brewers into the latest Murderer's Row. But a lineup filled with muscular home run types is no guarantee of a pennant. The 1947 Giants and 1956 Reds share the National League single season home run record at 221. The Giants finished fifth, the Reds third. The 1961 Yankees, however, romped to 109 victories in a year when they hit 240 homers, the major league record.

"You got to do with what you got in the park you play in," says Detroit manager Sparky Anderson, who managed Cincinnati's Big Red Machine of the mid-seventies, one of the most powerful teams in the game's history. "What I mean by that is, it don't do any good to play in a small park if you don't have guys who can hit it out of the park naturally. It don't do you any good to play in a big park if you don't have pitching, defense, and some speed. Put the 1975 Reds in Tiger Stadium and it would probably break all the records. Players have to learn to play within themselves, and teams that don't have the long-ballers have got to grind it out, play the percentages, and build a pitching staff."

The dominant teams of the 1980s will win with balance.

"It's tough to blow anybody away anymore," says Phillies manager Dallas Green, who brought that long-suffering town its only world champion-

Top: *Tommy Lasorda, the manager of the Los Angeles Dodgers, is not hesitant about expressing an opinion.*
Left: *Rickey Henderson played Billy Martin's brand of baseball for the A's in 1980 with 100 stolen bases.*

41

Right: *Atlanta's veteran pitcher, Phil Niekro, slaps a tag on Garry Maddox just as Garry hits first base for the Phillies.* Opposite: *This game between Billy Martin's Oakland A's and the Minnesota Twins seems to be up in the air. "Billy ball" will test 80s' defenses.*

42

ship in ninety-eight years with a 1980 blend of power, pitching, speed, and defense. "Everybody seems
to have enough pitching to shut your lineup down.
Everybody seems to have at least one bullpen stop-
per. I think we're going into a grind-it-out period
of baseball. To win, you gotta have a strong bench,
a good defense, speed to take the extra base when
it should be taken, and not be afraid to dirty your
uniform. There's very few clubs left—maybe Milwaukee—that can beat you consistently just swinging for the fences."

As baseball careens into the eighties, there is a

clear and present danger that a handful of teams
will become so dominant that competitive balance
will become as much of a mockery in the major
leagues as it is in the National Basketball Association, a faceless sprawl of franchises dominated by
Boston, Philadelphia, and Los Angeles.

The reason will not be rampant expansion into
unready markets, free agency or megabuck contracts. All those things can be dealt with within the
game's current parameters. What could turn the big
leagues into a half dozen Superteams and 20 surro-
gate sparring partners is the coming explosion of
Cable TV.

43

There were nights in the summer of 1980—many, in fact—when Ted Turner had more people watching his Braves perform in Anchorage, Alaska, than were scattered through the 52,000 seats of Atlanta's Fulton County Stadium. Let's hear it for The Superstation and the communications satellite off which it bounces its lucrative signal.

The wave of baseball's future is an airwave and Turner pointed the way to the big studio in outer space. Even if his latest and floundering All-News cable venture bankrupts him, National League owners smart enough to jump on the bandwagon early in the game will someday pay homage to Captain Outrageous the way Beatles fans revere the late John Lennon.

The Braves now come beaming into homes and motel rooms from sea to shining sea, in almost every community where cable TV franchises have been awarded. Hell, even a Superstation delayed-telecast of a Braves game at 1 A.M. beats a black-and-white "I Love Lucy" rerun, or "Give Us This Day." And if Turner's team ever gets good—championship good—the Dallas Cowboys may have company as America's Team.

The Phillies and Dodgers are among several National League teams to follow Turner's plunge into Cable TV. But there is a difference in approach. Turner sells you the Braves as part of the Channel 17 Superstation package. They are just another entry on the daily program log and don't generate any actual revenue for the Braves when measured against, say, their share of commercial network revenues.

The Phillies and Dodgers *sell* their games to Cable outlets and that is where the big bucks are going to be by the middle and end of the eighties. Really big bucks! Enough money for the teams who establish themselves in the Cable spinoffs early enough to dominate the game and buy a Dave Winfield or Fred Lynn a year.

"Next year," says Phillies vice-president Bill Giles, "we will take in more money from PRISM, our cable station, than we will from the networks. In 1983, we will be making more money on a per-game basis than we will from our local commercial TV contract. And I can see in the late eighties where we will make more money per game carried on pay cable TV than we will from our gate."

That's a mind-boggling projection right there. The Phillies' home average in 1980 was 33,996 paid admissions per game. That's an approximate gate of $175,000. The Phillies currently telecast about 25 PRISM games a year as an adjunct to their local

and network TV packages. So at 1981 prices and disallowing a certain increase in the number of cable games carried, Giles is talking about an additional $4.5 million in revenue, at the minimum.

Baseball for the rest of the decade will be dominated by the financial heavyweights—the Dodgers, Phillies, Astros, Expos, and Reds in the National League, the Yankees, Royals, and Angels in the American League.

The heavyweights will have the best of three worlds—independently wealthy ownership and more than enough income to fuel powerful farm systems and purchase outstanding free agent talent.

The handwriting is already on the wall for many teams who ignored the calendar and wasted their energies fighting lost battles against the toppling of the reserve clause and the emerging free agency.

It could take the Mets the rest of the decade to climb out of the long shadow cast by the Yankees in an interborough grapple for fans that is as one-sided as it is bitter. The Doubleday people might say the old magic is back, but it would help if they signed Mandrake the Magician to bat cleanup.

Even a team as recently dominant as the Pirates is slowly strangling in the harsh new economics. The Bucs, who lost $1 million in 1980, don't draw and don't command the TV revenues necessary to make up for a paucity of gate receipts. The Cubs have been a dead body for years, doomed more by organizational ineptitude than by the ability or unwillingness of their loyal fans to support the trip back into time that is Wrigley Field.

The Giants are hunkered down on that wind-blasted promontory midway between The City and the San Francisco Airport. Even with an inspired front office, which the Giants currently lack, one unassailable constant remains: Candlestick Park is baseball's Alcatraz. When the wind is howling in the right direction, you can almost hear attendance rising across the Bay in Oakland. The Bay area has proved it can't or won't support two major league baseball teams. The only question that remains is which one will move and when?

The geography which makes San Diego one of the last urban paradises on earth is also the Padres' worst enemy—Pacific to the west, desert to the east, Mexico to the south, and the sprawl of Los Angeles and Orange counties to the north, with wealthy teams located in each population core. San Diego County recently renamed its all-purpose stadium for Jack Murphy, a newspaper columnist who was the most influential voice in pushing through the stadium bond issue and bringing the Padres and NFL Chargers to town. Even Murphy, who passed away in the autumn of 1980, could not change the fact that there are barely one million people in San Diego County.

The Blue Collar bastions of Cleveland, Chicago, and Detroit have had depressed economies for years and the health of U.S. heavy industry and the quality of urban life in those cities will have a powerful influence on the ability of the Indians, White Sox, and Tigers to survive.

In the 1980s, the very rich will inherit the World Series rings.

Left to right: *Dusty Baker, Steve Garvey, Reggie Smith, and Ron Cey, the four sluggers for the Los Angeles Dodgers who each hit 30 or more home runs in the '78 season. The ends of the bats they are holding tell the story.*

4

Future Hall of Famers

Election to the Baseball Hall of Fame in the sleepy town of Cooperstown, New York, is the sport's equivalent of a Nobel prize, more valued in the retrospect of a man's career than even a World Series ring. Election to the Hall is neither easy nor automatic. A player does not become eligible for election until five seasons after his retirement. He must be named on 75 percent of more than 400 ballots cast by members of the Baseball Writers Association of America.

Only a few players of truly Olympian stature have been elected in their first year of eligibility, the most recent being former St. Louis Cardinal righthander Bob Gibson, the only player chosen in 1981. If a player has not been anointed in 15 years, his name is automatically removed from eligibility. His one remaining chance lies with the Veteran's Committee, which recently elected deserving but long neglected Hack Wilson and Chuck Klein to the Hall.

As major league baseball moved into the eighties, there were 13 active players whose careers had already produced the durability and statistical excellence mandatory for Hall of Fame consideration. Many were still at or near the peaks of long careers despite advancing age. The youngest of the group, Philadelphia third baseman Mike Schmidt, turned 31 shortly before winning the 1980 National League Most Valuable Player award. The oldest, Gaylord Perry, had signed a one-year contract with Atlanta at age 42 and needed just 11 victories to reach the magic 300 plateau.

Some of the Destined 13 will be elected on the first ballot—Pete Rose appears to have a lock on it. Others will wait several years for their 75 percent majority. All will eventually be enshrined.

Pete Rose

Pete Rose stormed angrily onto an elevator in the New York Sheraton Hotel. He grunted a greeting to Phillies' teammate John Vukovich. Then, without being asked the cause of his obvious pique,

Rose said, deliberately and clearly, "She filed."

Vukovich shrugged. He didn't quite catch Rose's drift. Who filed? Then it dawned on Rose's teammate. Pete's wife, Karolyn, had filed divorce papers in Cincinnati. Vukovich started to mumble something sympathetic, but Rose's voice cut him off. "Nothing to do now but go out and get some bleeping base hits," he said and waded through the crowded lobby to the waiting team bus.

The Phillies, preseason favorites to win the Eastern Division race in 1979 after signing celebrated free agent Rose for $3.5 million, were hopelessly mired in fourth place, victims of staggering injuries and a malaise of clubhouse dissension. Rose was 38 years old. He had nothing to drive him through a meaningless September but personal pride and a computer mind programming him toward a variety of goals and records.

On what should have been a bleak evening in his life, Rose shrugged off his personal problems and lashed four hits. He roared through September as if every pitcher was his enemy. When the smoke cleared, Rose had hit .421 for the final month with an incredible 51 hits. By the end of September he was working on a 23-game hitting streak and was pushing St. Louis first baseman Keith Hernandez for the batting title. The streak ended at 23 and he didn't catch Hernandez, but Rose finished the year with a .331 average, 208 hits, and a career-high 20 stolen bases.

As the 1981 All-Star Game approached, Rose was closing in on Stan Musial's National League record of 3,771 lifetime hits and fans were wondering if this remarkably durable man would threaten Ty Cobb's Himalayan total of 4,191.

In the 1970s, Rose missed only 15 games in 10 seasons and he has yet to miss a game in a Phillies uniform. What makes that feat even more remarkable is his reckless, head-first sliding style of play. "If he played for us," Philadelphia Eagles coach Dick Vermeil said after watching Rose perform in the 1980 World Series, "he'd be a linebacker."

Rose is also one of the most formidable mon-

Preceding pages: *Steve Carlton, durable lefthanded pitcher for the Philadelphia Phillies, won the Cy Young award for the third time in 1980, after a brilliant 24–9 season with 286 strikeouts and a 2.34 ERA.*

ey-making machines in baseball history. Although he never matched George Brett, Nolan Ryan, or Dave Winfield's $1 million-plus a-year salaries, Pete has reaped a lush harvest of endorsements in the off-season. During an autumn trip to Japan in 1979, Rose is believed to have lined up $250,000 in endorsements. And when he pursued Musial's National League record during the 1981 season, Pete used a rose-colored bat manufactured by Japan's giant Mizuno Corporation.

"I've never been blessed with home run power," he says. "I've never had great speed. But I'm a power hitter in that I hit a lot of doubles and I'm a great runner in that nobody runs the bases smarter than I do. I guess a lot of people don't consider me a great athlete because I don't look real smooth out there. But the name of the game is getting from home plate to first base and they don't give no prizes for how you look doing it."

Rose would like to manage when his career is over. He will surely approach that phase of the game with the same passionate, unswerving intensity.

Mike Schmidt

In a swimming pool, Michael Jack Schmidt can casually rip off the 100-yard freestyle in less than a minute. On a tennis court, despite minimal formal training, Schmidt holds his own at the club championship level of play. On a golf course, he wins the long drive trophy in nearly every tournament. On a basketball court, he looks at home scrimmaging with a powerhouse like the Philadelphia 76ers.

The fans saw this magnificently coordinated, 6-foot 2-inch, 205-pound athlete and they envisioned a man capable of hitting 60 home runs, driving in 150, batting .350, stealing 40 bases, and fielding his third base position better than any player before him.

No player in the modern era came to the game with greater all-around physical gifts. No player was more pressured by the fans—and his own—high expectations.

Schmidt will be forced to take more modest accomplishments with him to the Hall of Fame. He may be forced to live with the knowledge that instead of being the greatest all-around player of all time, he was merely the greatest all-around third baseman of all time. He never hit 60 homers, but by the time he reached the age of 31, Mike had led the majors in home runs four times. And in 1980, his 48 homers broke Eddie Mathews's single season

record for third basemen. He will never drive in 150 runs, but he has driven in more than 100 five times. He will never hit .350; his highest batting average going into the 1981 season was .286.

Schmidt has won five consecutive Gold Gloves at his position and he averages 15 stolen bases a season. Putting all the phases of his game together, Schmidt emerges as the best all-around player in the National League, flawed only in that the goals for his career were set too high.

"Schmitty sweats off more talent during a workout than most players have in a lifetime," Pete Rose says. "Once he realizes that nobody hits the ball hard every time up he can go about the business of being the best in the game."

A notorious streak hitter, Schmidt has no real explanation for the famines which so often follow feasts of awesome power hitting. "If I could answer that one I guess I could get rich just selling the information," he says. "So many little things go into a baseball swing—concentration, confidence, mechanics, patience, how you're feeling physically—that the slightest deviation from what you've been doing right can shut a hitter down. And you've gotta give pitchers some credit, too. They're out there making a living and when a guy is wearing them out, they've got to be smart enough to make some adjustments. I've had some awesome tears, no question of that. When I get in one of them, it's hard to picture not crushing the ball just about every time up. But when the slumps come it's just as hard to picture how anybody ever gets a hit in this game."

An athlete who keeps himself in superb condition all year, Schmidt should be a dominant player through the eighties. By the end of his marvelous career he should have at least 500 home runs.

Gaylord Perry

The Texas Rangers were having trouble giving Gaylord Perry away. They shopped him around at the 1977 winter meetings in Hawaii, but, hell, Gaylord was 39 years old and made a lot of money. Sure he was coming off a 15–12 season, but what were the odds of a pushing-40 pitcher repeating that kind of season? The Rangers were unable to unload Perry.

In mid-February, Texas general manager Eddie Robinson got a call from the San Diego Padres. Randy Jones, the Padres' 1976 Cy Young award winner, was coming off elbow surgery and the National League team desperately needed a veteran

pitcher to take up the slack while Jones fought to regain his winning form. The Rangers agreed—happily—to take an undistinguished lefthander named Dave Tomlin and $125,000 in cash for Perry. It was one of the greatest steals of the seventies.

Perry won 21 games. He lost only six. His earned run average was 2.72. Shortly after celebrating his fortieth birthday, Gaylord Jackson Perry won the Cy Young award, the first pitcher in history to win it in each major league.

Perry is a towering monument to the power of suggestion. Throughout his long career with seven teams, the 6-foot 4-inch righthander has been accused of throwing the illegal spitball (Perry actually applied a petroleum jelly to the ball), an act he has never strenuously denied. Hitters and umpires con-

stantly hawked his every move, trying to catch him in the act of applying the foreign substance to the baseball. The more they watched, the more distractions Perry added to his routine.

Peering in for the catcher's sign, he looked like a guy suffering from St. Vitas Dance, fingering the peak of his cap, running his fingers through his thinning hair, feeling around inside his glove. A master psychologist was at work. Having implanted the possibility of the spitball in the hitter's mind, Gaylord would throw a sinker, slider, or changeup and record another out.

Actually, he had used the illegal pitch sparingly during his career with the Giants, reserving it for critical situations where he needed a strikeout or ground ball. The pitch is extremely hard on the arm

and people tend to forget that Perry's legal assortment of pitches was superb. His career strikeout total of more than 3,300 is sufficient testimony to the man's skill and pitching knowledge.

Perry went into the 1980 reentry draft as a free agent and was signed by Ted Turner's Atlanta Braves needing just 11 more victories to reach the magic 300 total for his career. "I think a pitcher that close to three hundred should get a chance to do it," Turner said. "But the main reason I signed him is that I think the man is still a helluva pitcher who can help the Braves win a pennant."

Steve Carlton

He stopped talking to the media for good during the 1978 season after years of selected boycotts aimed at a broad spectrum of writers. He is moody, egotistical, rude, superstitious, and stubborn. The closeup TV camera reveals a face aswarm with nervous ticks. In an age when few players read anything heavier than *People* magazine, he devours works of Oriental philosophy. In an era when the favored clubhouse beverage remains beer, he celebrates victories with a quiet glass of estate-bottled French wine—quite possibly from an estate he visited personally.

He does not care to be in crowded places. So to insure the sanctity of the space he demands in life, he packs his ears with wads of cotton when he pitches—insulation from the roar of the crowd.

Steven Norman Carlton is different from you

51

and me. He dances to a sitar only he hears. But his lone wolf posture and total disdain for the print media has not kept him from his appointed innings. Carlton slogs in solitary splendor toward his place among the greatest lefthanders in baseball history.

Carlton powered to his third Cy Young award in 1980, a season when he was so dominant an award should have been given to the best of the rest. The Schuykill Sphinx was 24–9 with an earned run average of 2.34. His 286 strikeouts were over 100 more than the second most productive power pitcher in the majors.

But Carlton will never have a season to match 1972, when he accounted for 43 percent of the sixth-place Phillies' victories. Carlton was 27–10 with a 1.98 ERA and struck out 310 hitters in 346 innings pitched. He will probably be remembered as much for his amazing durability as for his superb fastball, slider, and curve.

In his first 14 full seasons with the Cardinals and Phillies, the student of Oriental martial arts averaged 271 innings pitched per season.

"Hitting Steve Carlton is like trying to eat soup with a fork," Willie Stargell once muttered. "When his slider is on there ain't a hitter on the planet who can touch it."

Although the Phillies of the late seventies had an all-star catcher in Bob Boone, Carlton refused to pitch to anybody but his old Cardinal teammate Tim McCarver. This arrangement added two years to McCarver's long career and gave him the unique opportunity to serve as Carlton's press secretary. Tim fielded all questions about Lefty's performance during postgame interviews while the pitcher sequestered himself in an off-limits sanctuary. Some of McCarver's lines are memorable.

"When Lefty and I die," he said in 1978, "we want to be buried sixty feet, six inches apart. Lefty wants a resin bag on his tombstone. I want a catcher's mask."

On another occasion, McCarver feigned anger. "I caught Steve cheating," Timmy huffed. "He was showering with one of the other catchers. I'm filing for divorce."

Writers chronicling Steve Carlton's Harpo Marx career needed all the laughs they could get.

Willie Stargell

It was raining gently and the Three Rivers Stadium infield was covered. In three hours, the Phillies and 1979 World Champion Pirates would tangle in a key September game.

The field was deserted. The stands were empty. Then Wilver Dornell Stargell emerged from the Pittsburgh clubhouse with veteran teammate Grant Jackson. For the better part of an hour, Stargell and Jackson played pepper behind the batting cage, the lefthanded pitcher tossing the ball gently to the big bear of a man; Stargell caressing the ball back to Jackson.

They played their lonely little game in the gathering early autumn twilight. There would be no more baseball for Stargell in 1980. His knees were shot and Pirates fans could chart the fall of their team to third place from the August day when Stargell went on the disabled list. The Stargell-Jackson tableau in the rain took on a note of exquisite nostalgia when the stadium sound system erupted with the hand-clapping, foot-stomping refrain of "Fam-i-lee," the Sister Sledge anthem the Pirates rallied around during the championship drive the year before.

Other sluggers will go the Hall of Fame with more imposing numbers than those Willie Stargell compiled during a career which brought him to Pittsburgh in 1962. But no player ever represented a city with more style, grace, or sense of obligation. In a blue collar city, a town where a majority of the fans work in heavy industry, they could identify with Stargell, their powerful, aging first baseman.

By the time he went on the disabled list in 1980, Stargell had pounded out 472 career home runs. But he didn't become a truly national figure until 1979, when his memorable October slugging set a city afire and captured America's imagination.

The 1971 Pirates would not have won the pennant without what Stargell considers his finest season. He picked them up on his broad back and carried them, leading the National League with 48 homers and driving in 125 runs in just 141 games.

But the postseason belonged to the late Roberto Clemente, whose dazzling play against the favored Baltimore Orioles dominated the World Series. Clemente deserved the accolades, but Stargell's .208 average in the Series detracted unfairly from the luster of a magnificent season.

That was not the case in 1979 when Stargell, weary from playing every day down the stretch of a torrid race with the Montreal Expos, shrugged off his advancing years and unfurled three weeks of unsurpassed postseason slugging.

"When you get into the playoffs and World Series there's no such thing as being tired," Stargell said on the eve of the championship series with the Western Division champion Reds. "This is what the whole long season is all about. This is what a professional baseball player lives for."

Stargell batted .455 with two homers and six RBI in the Pirates three-game sweep of the Reds. And in the Fam-i-lee's comeback from a 1–3 deficit in the World Series against the Orioles, Pops was stupendous, setting new Series records with 25 total bases and seven extra base hits.

At the age of 38, Stargell shared the 1979 MVP award with St. Louis first baseman Keith Hernandez, recognition many felt was long overdue for an elder statesman who served his game so long and well.

Steve Garvey

Steve Garvey would have been perfect for the 1950s, when short hair, respect for authority, and strong family ties were still admired characteristics.

Instead, Garvey came to baseball in the 1970s. The antihero was in vogue. Because he spoke of his profession in glowing terms, cooperated with the press, signed autographs for youngsters, got on well with his employers, played with consistent enthusiasm and married a dazzling blond of similar apple pie qualities, Garvey was often viewed by his peers with sullen disdain.

His "straight" image was sneered at by several Los Angeles Dodger teammates. During the 1980 season, his marriage was placed under a microscope by a national sports magazine to an extent so brutal that Steve and Cindy Garvey sought relief in the courts.

Despite his good-guy image, Garvey managed to be one of the most durable and consistent first basemen in baseball history. Just 32 at the start of the 1981 season, the former Michigan State all-American defensive back hadn't missed a game since 1976, a streak of durability unmatched in the modern era even by Pete Rose.

"A lot of the detractors who are always ready to knock Steve Garvey couldn't carry his shoelaces as a man or as competitors," says Tommy Lasorda, his manager. "He's the kind of guy who has made America great and don't forget it."

The pitchers won't forget it. And the Dodgers won't forget his unselfishness. From the time Garvey became the regular first baseman in 1974, he was a line drive, contact hitter, who sacrificed power for batting average.

He strung together .312, .319, and .317 seasons. But in 1977, Lasorda felt his offense was in a rut. The Dodgers needed more runs than they were producing with a hunt-and-peck attack.

"I talked to Steve in spring training and told him he had the power to hit at least twenty-five home runs," Lasorda said. "I said his average would probably suffer but it was important to the offense for him to hit more long balls."

As Lasorda predicted, Garvey's average tailed off to .297. But the manager sold his first baseman short in the power department. Garvey slammed 33 homers and drove in a career-high 115 runs. It was the first season, however, in which he failed to collect 200 hits. Over a span of seven seasons beginning in 1974, Garvey has averaged 201 hits.

OK, he never made it as an antihero. Charles Manson is safe. Steve Garvey never cursed a sportswriter, snarled at a small child seeking an autograph, or wound up in a spring training drunk tank.

The Hall of Fame will probably take him anyway.

Reggie Jackson

It says something for the considerable ego of Reginald Martinez Jackson that after Muhammad Ali's final fall from the athletic limelight against heavyweight champion Larry Holmes, the latest Pride of the Yankees volunteered to assume Ali's role as world spokesman for the black man.

Jackson has been a bigger-than-life personality for more than a decade. He is a newsmaker, a moneymaker, and a home-run maker. Modesty does not become him and Reggie, Reggie, Reggie has never tried very hard to duck the spotlight.

Purists will argue that Jackson's career statistics are somewhat less than Cooperstown caliber, that his average is too low and his strikeouts too frequent.

But he is a home run hitter in the classic, modern sense. There is nothing compromising about his swing, a majestic, from-the-butt assault on the baseball that threatens to separate his arms from his powerful torso. Only Babe Ruth and Mickey Mantle were able to strike out with an equal combination of majesty and menace.

After his celebrated free agent signing with the Yankees following a brilliant career in Oakland and one-year sabbatical in Baltimore, Reggie became a leading man in a daily Yankee Stadium morality play titled, "The Bronx Zoo."

During the Yankees' noisy run to the 1977 World Series title, Jackson and manager Billy Martin took turns savaging each other in the newspa-

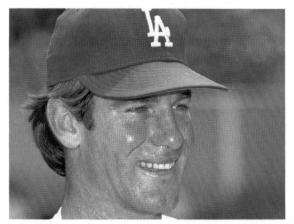

pers, a sustained barrage of vitriol almost without parallel in the game's history. It was terrific theater and everybody loved it, including owner George Steinbrenner, who knew the value of a headline.

But Jackson was undeniably worth his enormous salary. He helped restore to refurbished Yankee Stadium the glory that was Ruth and the grandeur that was DiMaggio. And his dues were paid in full when he set a World Series record in game six against the Dodgers. Reggie hammered three home runs, the final one a 450-foot shot to right center off knuckleballer Charley Hough. He had earned his nickname, "Mr. October."

Jackson silenced some of the critics in 1980 by unfurling his finest all-around season. Jackson hit .300 on the button, 41 homers, second highest total of his career, and drove in 111 runs.

It was a solid enough performance to propel Jackson into another dizzying run of lucrative national TV product endorsements, including the classic "Reggie-Vision" series for the Panasonic Corporation.

A brilliant running back at Philadelphia's Cheltenham High School, Jackson wisely chose

baseball at Arizona State, a college which offered him scholarships for either sport.

His charisma, wit, intelligence, and flair for the dramatically correct would have been wasted on the once-a-week stage of pro football. Reggie Jackson never bored fans with false humility. Here is how he began his 1975 autobiographical diary, *Reggie:*

"My name is Reggie Jackson and I am the best in baseball . . ."

And that's Reggie vision.

Rod Carew

In his final at bat of the 1960 season, Ted Williams hit a 425-foot home run into the distant right-center bullpen in Boston's Fenway Park and called it a career. Williams left behind him a .344 lifetime batting average and 521 career home runs. One can only speculate what records he would have shattered had he played in 1943–45 and in 1952–53.

Williams served in World War II and Korea as a Marine fighter pilot. The greatest hitter of the modern era missed 727 games in the prime of his

career and the mind boggles at what he would have achieved had he played during those seasons. By even the most conservative yardstick, Williams missed 2,500 at bats, which translates into 170 home runs when you figure he hit a homer every 14.7 at bats.

But Williams was brittle. He had fewer than 3,000 hits in those 19 seasons. He played every game in only one season.

Which brings us to the greatest hitter of the current era, Rodney Cline Carew, a slender, underpublicized infielder born in the shadow of the great Gatun lock in Panama.

"He's the best pure hitter in the game," said Gene Mauch, the man who managed Carew in Minnesota during the late 1970s. "And he's the best bunter in this history of the game. The little man has a magic bat."

Although never confused with the great power hitters of his time, Rod is off by himself when measured against his contemporaries in batting average and base hit production.

"I'm strong enough to hit home runs, but that style would have been counterproductive," Carew has said. "My style has been to hit the ball to all fields and capitalize on my speed."

Carew has won seven American League batting titles since 1969. His .388 average and 239 hits in 1977 were the peak performance by a major leaguer since Williams also hit .388 in 1957. But Williams had only 420 at bats that season and barely qualified for the batting title.

Fans of Kansas City star George Brett are reminded that his .390 average in 1980 was accomplished in only 449 at bats. When Carew hit .388 he went to the plate 616 times!

Rod harvested the fruits of potential free agency after announcing he would not sign a 1979 contract with the pinch-penny Twins. Rather than lose their star without compensation, the Twins traded him to the California Angels for a handful of undistinguished players. But the durable first baseman suffered the first serious injury of his career and appeared in only 110 games for the Western Division champions.

Brett's assault on .400 obscured a marvelous comeback by Carew during the 1980 season. Rod batted a solid .331, very close to his career average of .333.

The day after his trade to the Angels, a friend of club batting coach Deron Johnson asked the obvious. What in the world does a batting coach tell a man who has won seven batting titles?

Deron pondered the question a few moments. "I'll tell him to bat lefthanded," he shrugged.

Don Sutton

The 1980 division races were at full boil. In the Western Division of the National League, the Dodgers were nipping at the heels of the Houston Astros. In the Eastern Division, the Phillies were battling to overtake the Pirates and Expos.

A Friday night crowd of nearly 50,000 was in Dodger Stadium for the start of the first weekend in September and they saw a game that will remain etched on their memories, the summer game at its best, a classic pitching duel between Steve Carlton and Don Sutton.

Carlton was overpowering; Sutton the consummate nibbler who used a variety of speeds and every inch of the plate as well as the area around it.

It was Sutton's finest performance of the season. He outdueled Carlton, 1–0, in a game the Dodgers had to win, and struck out 10, a season high for Tommy Lasorda's pitching staff.

"Gentlemen, tonight you saw the Mona Lisa being painted out there," the theatrical Lasorda said. "The Phillies' guy was great, but my guy was greater."

Sutton was a violinist among fiddlers as a 20-year-old rookie in 1966. "He appears to be wise beyond his years," said Hall of Fame manager Walter Alston, a master of understatement. Sutton never pitched with the awesome power of Sandy Koufax or the intimidating efficiency of Don Drysdale, but he plugged along, piling one good season on top of another.

When the blithe spirit from Clio, Alabama, finished the 1980 season with 230 career victories, he had more lifetime wins than any pitcher in the history of the illustrious organization, more strikeouts than Koufax, and the considerable clout of free agency.

Incredibly, the Dodgers, who had been burned to a crisp by their refusal to meet the salary demands of lefthanded ace Tommy John two years before, made no effort to sign Sutton after the 1980 reentry draft. A lively bidding war ensued and Sutton emerged from it with a five-year $4.5 million contract offered by the already pitching-rich Houston Astros.

"I think I have the stuff and the arm to pitch effectively for five more years," Sutton said. "I've had a tendency to throw a lot of home run balls in the past and I think the dimensions of the Astrodome will be in my favor. If they start jacking homers out of there on me I'll be in trouble."

Sutton is another master of mound intrigue. For years he's been accused of putting extra sink on his sinker and slide on his slider by cutting or scuffing the ball. The mystery has always been how he accomplished the act of desecrating the ball's smooth surface.

Phillies manager Danny Ozark, who had been a Dodger coach, blew the whistle on Sutton. "He files one of the grommet holes in his glove to razor sharpness," Danny said. "It's sharp enough to make a tiny cut on the ball, just enough to make it do a little extra. But he's like Gaylord Perry. He'll save it for when he really needs it. Half the times when hitters have asked the umpire to examine the ball, Don will have thrown a normal pitch. The power of suggestion is great once a pitcher lets a hitter know he *can* do something to the ball."

The ball Sutton sends to the Hall of Fame is guaranteed to be unsullied.

Carl Yastrzemski

He was already a veteran, an American League batting champion, when he staged what his manager, Dick Williams, still calls, "the greatest sustained performance I've ever seen by a baseball player."

The year was 1967. The Red Sox were coming off a last place finish and Carl Yastrzemski spent the winter insuring that he wouldn't repeat a dismal .278 performance. He realized he was resting on his laurels, that he wasn't physically or mentally attuned to the rigors demanded of a championship performance. Under the direction of a wispy Hungarian fitness expert named Gene Berde, Yaz turned his body into an iron bar, purged his mind of defeatist thoughts, and he went out and gave Red Sox fans a season to remember.

Yastrzemski won the Triple Crown, batting .326 with 44 homers and 121 RBI. During a tense stretch race with the Minnesota Twins, the leftfielder from Notre Dame seemed to compress all his skills. At the end, in two vital games against the Twins, he went 7-for-8 and every ball came whooshing off his bat like a shell from a howitzer. He played the celebrated "Green Monster," Fenway Park's rococo left field fence, the way Heifetz played a violin. And after the Red Sox clinched their first pennant in two decades, Yaz stood in the cramped Fenway clubhouse atop two folding chairs

and told the swarming press mob that it had been fun, "like playing stickball in the streets."

In 1975, a preseason publication noted, "Carl Yastrzemski, still a quality hitter at thirty-five, [is] no longer able to deliver the long ball consistently . . ."

Since that premature burial of his skills, Yaz has cranked out an additional 116 homers and added 482 RBI to his career total. In the spring of 1981, Yaz reported to the Red Sox Winter Haven, Florida, training camp for the twenty-first time,

Steve Carlton is a loner. He doesn't grant interviews to the press, preferring to let his record speak for itself. That record is eloquent, revealing one of the greatest lefthanders in the history of baseball.

still a factor in the club's offensive scheme as its lefthanded designated hitter.

His skill as an all-around player came into focus in the final game of the Red Sox three-game playoff sweep of the defending champion A's. Reggie Jackson was the tying run when he came up to face Rick Wise in the eighth inning. The all-star Oakland leader hit a searing liner to left center. It would be a gapper, a double or triple which would score two runs and put the A's back in the hunt. Yaz came from nowhere. He reached back into his youth and found the swiftness and strength to make one more incredible play. He raced into the gap, dove, and somehow kept the ball from going through. Only one run scored. Jackson settled for a single. Dick Drago relieved Wise and ended the threat with a doubleplay grounder.

"Superstars do unthinkable things," Jackson said graciously after Boston clinched the pennant. "I've been watching Yaz do them since I've been in the majors. When the money was down he played like a superstar. He dominated the playoff. He beat

Opposite: *Rod Carew is headed for the Hall with a*
lifetime average of .333 and seven batting titles.
Above: *Don Sutton uses psychology and finesse as he*
burns batters and turns in one good year after another.

us with his bat, his glove, his head, and his heart. My hat is off to the man. He took away my money, but he didn't steal it. He earned it."

Jim Palmer

Jim Palmer models Jockey shorts and fights a lot with his manager, Earl Weaver. You probably already knew that.

Jim Palmer is also one of the best righthanders in baseball history. You probably already knew that, too, even though Palmer has spent his entire career pitching for the Baltimore Orioles, a team which receives a minimum of national publicity. Women know who Palmer is, though. He's the hunk in the underwear ad with looks in the Robert Redford league.

And handsome does as handsome is. Going into the 1981 season, Palmer's career record was 241–132. Only a sore arm in 1974 kept him from stringing together what would have been a record 9 straight seasons of 20 or more victories. As it was 8 out of 9 wasn't bad. But almost as entertaining as Palmer's consistent mastery of American League hitters has been his love-hate relationship with Weaver, the feisty little pepper-pot who has been his only big league manager. They may be growing old together, but they sure as hell haven't mellowed.

Weaver and his star see eye-to-eye on almost nothing. If Palmer told Weaver it was high noon, Earl would grumble an obscenity and order the groundskeeper to turn on the lights. A lot of the contention revolves around Weaver's unshakable belief that Palmer is the number-one hypochondriac to ever pull on a big league uniform.

Earl, who plays Don Rickles to Palmer's Rodney Dangerfield in an act that would sell out in Las Vegas, measures his seasons with the Orioles by Jim's injuries.

"There was the Year of the Back, the Year of the Elbow, the Year of the Shoulder, and, oh yeah, the Year of the Ulna Bone," Weaver likes to recite with rich sarcasm. "Well, that's the way he refers to it anyway."

Palmer's "Poor Soul" routines are no less entertaining. When the Orioles were driving for the 1979 pennant, Jim regaled the press with this routine: "Why did I never leave Baltimore? Because I was dumb. I was dumb enough to believe I'd be rewarded for my service here. I know I'm not worth the money a Pete Rose gets. He plays every day. But I do feel I should be getting a salary similar to what other pitchers who have accomplished less than me are getting. But the Orioles say they can't afford it."

It's been going on like that in Baltimore since 1968, when Weaver was named manager at midseason. But Weaver slips out of the James Cagney role once in a while and reveals his true feelings for Palmer. "I've won one thousand two-hundred games as a manager here," he says, "and Jim's won about a fifth of them. Without his two hundred forty-one wins I wouldn't even be standing here talking to you. I probably would have been fired years ago."

The Jim and Earl Show is currently in its fourteenth season, as enduring as the "Ziegfeld Follies" or George White's "Scandals." Palmer says he isn't feeling too well, but he'll probably be able to stagger out there for his next start. "I thought he was through in 1967," said Weaver. "The man's arm was shot. Done! That was about two hundred twenty victories ago. I just wish he'd go out and pitch and let me worry about running the ballclub."

Johnny Bench

Sparky Anderson, the baseball manager, is a master of hyperbole, a positive thinker who could make winning a World Series sound better than the invention of a cancer cure. But Sparky wasn't hyping the truth too extravagantly when he said this about Johnny Bench, the catcher of the seventies:

"I say that God came down and touched Johnny Bench's mother and said, 'I'm going to give you the most talented baseball player ever born.'"

Bench was raised in an Oklahoma town that could have been the set for *The Last Picture Show.* God may have fallen short of producing history's greatest baseball player when he created Bench, but he made sure John would earn his fame.

Bench survived a teen-age bus wreck that killed two of his teammates. His brilliant career was almost ended by a lesion on a lung. He has suffered shoulder, rib, and chronic back problems and the ballyhoo of a 1976 divorce from high-fashion model Vicky Chesser. The persistent injuries, badges of the catching trade, kept him from achieving the statistical greatness predicted for him when he broke in with the Reds in 1968 and caught 154 games in his first full National League season. But the big numbers started coming in 1970, when he slammed 45 homers and drove in 148 runs, a performance which earned him the first of two MVP awards.

Bench never dominated the game, but he was

Jim Palmer, pitching ace for the Baltimore Orioles, has movie star looks and a 241–132 lifetime record going into 1981. His ongoing battles with the feisty Earl Weaver have never reached the point of no return.

Opposite top: *Carl Yastrzemski is one of the most durable and consistent players to hit for the Red Sox and guard the "Green Monster" in Fenway Park's left field.*
Opposite bottom: *The Reds' Tom Seaver knows he's throwing correctly if he dips low enough to get dirt on his right knee.* Left: *Jim Palmer pitches commercials when he's not on the mound.* Below: *Johnny Bench has "soft hands" and a tough bat.*

63

the best there was at the game's most difficult position for more than a decade and he began a new life as an outfielder in the 1981 season, a move he hoped would prolong his career.

He starred for the Reds at a time when Steve Carlton was the National League's premier lefthander. Bench displayed some measure of his ability to rise to an occasion by hitting three home runs in one game off Carlton not once, but twice. "When they send one of Lefty's baseball's to the Hall of Fame," Tim McCarver once quipped, "one of Bench's bats will be waiting there to smoke it."

The 1976 World Series, a four-game Reds annihilation of the Yankees, provided Bench with his greatest personal thrill. He batted .533 and buried the Yankees in the final game with two homers and five RBI in a 7–2 Reds victory.

"This performance tonight is my best," he said after receiving the Series MVP award. "I've hit three homers in a game before but this is my best. I was emotionally high in that I didn't do well in my last Series."

He will be remembered for his slugging, but baseball men seem to agree that Bench was probably the finest technical catcher of all time. "Nobody ever handled pitchers better, threw out runners better, or blocked the plate better," Sparky Anderson said.

God got that much of the assignment right.

Tom Seaver

The date was April 1, 1966, and a 21-year-old pitcher named Tom Seaver had a very real problem. The NCAA, the body which governs college athletics, had just declared that Tom was no longer eligible to pitch for Southern Cal. Why? Seaver had just signed a contract with the Atlanta Braves which would go into effect at the end of June, when his class graduated.

It was a problem because Seaver was caught in the middle. He could neither compete for the University of Southern California nor report to spring training with the Braves. Seaver was in limbo and he appealed to General William Eckert, the Unknown Soldier who served one year as commissioner of baseball. Seaver complained that the situation left him in the twilight zone, and asked baseball to work something out in his behalf.

In one of the few rulings of his brief tenure, Eckert decreed that the Braves had acted improperly and that Seaver could now sign for the same $50,000 bonus with any other club that showed in-

terest. Looking back on Seaver's marvelous career, it is amazing but true that only three clubs—the Indians, Phillies, and Mets threw their hats in the ring. And the Phillies never followed up their expression of interest. Eckert decreed that the three clubs should draw from a hat. The Mets drew out Seaver's name and the rest is history.

Handsome, urbane, and articulate, Seaver became a matinee idol in New York and one of the finest righthanded pitchers of his era. And when he helped pitch the Miracle Mets of 1969 to that improbable World Series title over the Baltimore Orioles, Seaver became a national hero. Talk all you want about the Dallas Cowboys, the 1969 Mets were the original "America's team."

Pitching for a team that frequently scored runs in clusters of one and none, Seaver is a five-time winner of 20 or more games, a three-time Cy Young award recipient, and five-time National League strikeout king. Before injuries took the zip off his fastball and the snap off his curve and slider, Tom was a Spalding Guide righthander, a man who performed with a great integrity of style. He was a consummate power pitcher whose straightforward, challenging delivery reminded purists of Hall of Famer Robin Roberts.

"He's very comfortable to hit against," says Phillies slugger Mike Schmidt. "You know he's going to be right around the plate, you know he's coming right at you. But he's so damn good it's very hard to hit the ball. I guess you could say Tom doesn't make you feel as bad after you strike out as some pitchers."

Seaver was the central figure in one of the most publicized trades of the 1970s. Unable to reach agreement with the thrifty Mets on a long-term contract in negotiations frequently conducted in the newspapers, Seaver was traded to the powerful Cincinnati Reds on June 15, 1977, for a package of players that did nothing to improve the Mets' sagging fortunes. The trade left many Mets fans bitter and attendance dropped dramatically. Few New York fans will forget Seaver's 1969 performance, when he was 25–7.

Tom pitched well for the Reds, despite frequent lower back and arm problems aggravated by his tremendous leg action when driving off the mound. He spent long stretches of the 1980 season on the disabled list, but still managed to finish with a 10–8 record and went into his fifteenth big league season with a lifetime record of 245–143. His lifetime winning percentage of .631 is the highest of any active pitcher.

5

5

Play Ball!

Preceding pages: *Versatile Steve Garvey plays the Man for All Positions for the Los Angeles Dodgers. Here he waits for a throw at third base as the runner does a Pete Rose slide.* Above: *The efficient ground crew for the Mets smoothes the infield between innings at Shea Stadium.* Opposite: *No suburban lawn gets the meticulous grooming and tender loving care that Baltimore's ground crew gives the Memorial Stadium turf.*

68

Above: *Don Baylor, now with the California Angels, concentrates on the pitch in a hit-and-run situation.* Left: *The New York Mets' Elliot Maddox shows perfect form as he prepares to lay down a bunt.* Opposite: *Gene Richards, outfielder for the San Diego Padres, had an outstanding season in 1980 with a .301 batting average. Richards collected 193 hits in 642 at bats over 158 games, and stole a very respectable 61 bases.*

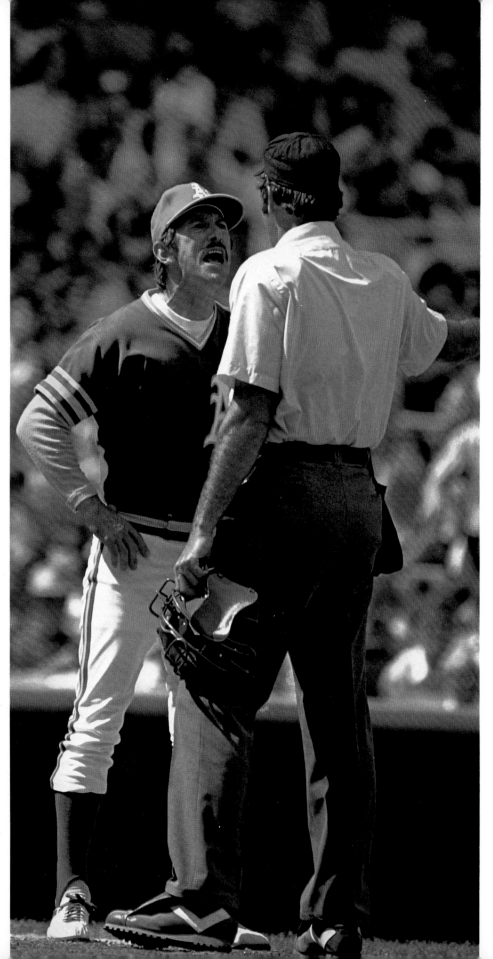

Preceding pages: *Hitting a baseball rocketing to the plate at speeds approaching 100 m.p.h. has been described as the most difficult act in sport.* Opposite: *Gifted debater Los Angeles manager Tommy Lasorda has some choice and completely reasonable observations to make to an unsympathetic ump.* Left: *Billy Martin, chief of the Oakland A's, stands up to the face of adversity.*

Above: *Fans have
undampened enthusi-
asm in wet weather.*
Right: *The Summer
Game is enjoyed by
fans of all ages.*
Opposite: *These
Chicago White Sox
fans say that this
year is "the Year."*

76

Preceding pages: *Larry Bowa makes a hardnosed play at second for the Phillies as he gets the throw off under pressure from the base runner who is attempting to break up the play.* Above: *New faces—a ball girl for the Toronto Bluejays.* Right: *Bill Russell (18) is there first on a pop fly to the L.A. infield.* Opposite: *This right-handed San Francisco batter makes some quick adjustments to get out of the way of a brush-back pitch. The fine line between brushing and beaning has caused more than one brawl.*

80

Right: *Tim Foley turns the double play at second for Pittsburgh, avoiding the sliding runner as he throws.* Below: *Sometimes the pitcher loses a little control and the batter has to skip rope.* Opposite: *It's the job of the base runner to break up the double play at second and his spikes are the tools used for the task.*

It has frequently been said that the game of baseball is a game of inches. Here, the runner has executed a perfect fadeaway slide, and has managed to keep a foot on the bag. The Baltimore infielder has his right foot in poor position, and the final result is "safe!"

6

Ten for the Eighties

To an explorer, the horizon he has traveled from contains more certainties than the one which lies ahead. The Hall of Fame candidates of the previous chapter are old, established firms, athletes who journeyed with us through the 1970s, leaving in their wake a litter of accomplishments. Some will continue near the peak level of their skills deep into this decade.

It is difficult to assemble a list of 10 players who will deliver to the fans the same consistency and excellence they got from Pete Rose and Carl Yastrzemski, Steve Carlton and Willie Stargell, Jim Palmer and Steve Garvey. The rules of the game remain essentially those of our fathers and grandfathers. But the economics of the game have changed dramatically. Many players have grown very rich at a very young age. They are products of a commodities market, where future expectations often outweigh past performance. In the winter of 1980, Dave Winfield, a 29-year-old outfielder, became a free agent after playing out his option with the San Diego Padres. He came out of a four-team bidding war with a staggering, 10-year contract variously estimated to be worth between $15 million and $25 million. The average wage earner simply cannot comprehend an athlete earning that kind of money to play a game invented to occupy the leisure time of rural children.

Even more boggling than the sheer weight of numbers is the fact that during the first eight years of his career, Winfield's accomplishments were decidedly underwhelming. His average edged over the .300 mark only twice. He hit as many as 30 homers and drove in as many as 100 runs only once. These are minimal numbers when used for comparison with the standard criteria for baseball greatness. But Yankee owner George Steinbrenner has the money to spend and wanted the best free agent outfielder available.

Baseball is making a curious passage through an era when the best players are rarely the highest paid. When Mike Schmidt signed a five-year contract at $565,000 a year in 1978, the Phillies third baseman was briefly the game's highest paid player. By the end of 1980's free agent signings, at least 10 players were earning more per season than the man who was the National League's Most Valuable Player. In fact, Garry Maddox, an outfielder known chiefly for his defensive ability, signed a long-term contract during the 1980 season calling for more than $700,000 a year.

If a Winfield was worth $1.5 million a year then, what will a Schmidt be worth in 1982?

The stars of this decade will need more than raw skill. They will need a sense of pride and obligation which transcends the length and breadth of their incredible contracts. How many will have the strength of character to play with a nagging injury, knowing their salary is guaranteed whether they play or not? How many athletes playing out their option seasons will jeopardize a multimillion-dollar contract down the road by running into an outfield fence or crunching head-first into a catcher at home plate?

Will the star of the eighties earn his fantastic salary with the sweat of honest toil, or will it become known as the Decade of the Dog?

The 10 players chosen here as the most likely to dominate the decade are all everyday performers. Big league pitching is at the end of a 15-year cycle and the men who will win Cy Young awards for the rest of the decade have yet to identify themselves.

George Brett

In 1973, a lefthanded pitcher named Ken Brett did something no player at his position had ever done before, something no pitcher has done since, or is likely to do in the future. Brett, a handsome journeyman from a family of baseball-playing brothers, homered in four consecutive games in which he was the starting pitcher.

But the record book lies. A myopic second base umpire deprived him of a home run in a fifth consecutive game, losing track of a 415-foot shot over the center field cyclone fence in San Francis-

Preceding pages: *Willie Wilson, speed burner for the Kansas City Royals, starts his slide at third as the Phillies' Mike Schmidt covers the bag in the 1980 World Series. The Phillies took the Series.*

co's Candlestick Park. Brett was awarded a ground rule double when the umpire ruled the ball had gone over the fence on a bounce. "It cleared the fence by at least ten feet on the fly," centerfielder Garry Maddox admitted afterward. "No doubt, it was a home run." Throughout his record home run streak for a pitcher, Kenny consistently downplayed his hitting prowess.

"I've got a little brother named George who's going to be the hitter in the family," Ken said.

George Brett was at Omaha that season and hit an unspectacular .284 for the Kansas City Royals' Triple A club. The Royals called him up in September and he hit a pressing 5-for-40—hardly the stats of a future batting champion.

In 1976, George Brett led the American League with a .333 average. He also led the league in hits (215), triples (14), and total bases (298).

In 1980, George Brett got serious about his hitting. For the better part of an injury-plagued season, the aggressive third baseman flirted with the first .400 average by a major league regular since Ted Williams rang up a .406 mark in 1941.

The injuries took their toll, though. Brett was hobbled much of September with a painful hand injury and finished the season with a mere .390 average and just enough at bats to qualify him for his second batting title. But the highest average in 39 years excited fans the way they hadn't been excited since 1978, when Pete Rose chased Joe DiMaggio's Olympian 56-game hitting streak. When George raised his average over .400 during a torrid August, he became a media event and he handled the constant barrage of interviews with style and grace.

More important, George Brett led the Royals to their first pennant, a performance which earned him the MVP award despite sensational seasons by Reggie Jackson and Milwaukee's Cecil Cooper. But future historians will have difficulty discerning which facet of his season received greater notoriety, the .390 average or a hemorrhoid condition which flared before the first game of the World Series. Amid an avalanche of bad bathroom jokes, an off-feed Brett helped keep his team competitive in a Series the Royals lost in six games.

Just 28, George Brett has a chance to be baseball's dominant all-around hitter for the balance of the decade. But a lack of durability could do more to keep his skyrocketing career in check than any combination of pitchers.

In sickness and in health, Brett has already proved he will not be outworked. He studies his art with the intensity and single-mindedness which

made Williams a legend in his approach to hitting a speeding baseball. On a scorching afternoon in August during his .390 season, Brett showed up at Royals Stadium at 2:30 in the afternoon to study old films of Babe Ruth batting. "I wanted to watch his top hand come off the bat," Brett explained.

Then he went out into the 105-degree heat and took extra hitting. Was he trying to battle out of a slump? Nah, George was working on a 27-game streak. The night before he had gone 4-for-5, including a homer and two doubles. Extra hitting? Brett was fuming over the single out he had made.

"I swung at a bad pitch," he said with the despondent air of a man involved in some deep failure. "I should have more confidence. He came inside three pitches in a row. Why didn't I look for the fourth one? Why am I defensive when I'm hot?" With his head back in the proper offensive gear, George went out that night and went 2-for-2. Practice makes perfect.

"The only way to stop him is inside," says Yankee lefthander Rudy May. "That way, he's got to pull the ball and you don't have to worry about getting drilled with a line drive."

Orioles manager Earl Weaver prides himself on the book he has on rival hitters. But Earl says he has no sage advice to offer his pitchers when they go against George Brett. "I tell 'em they're on their own," Weaver shrugs.

"There's no way to get the guy out when he's in his groove," Phillies manager Dallas Green said after the World Series. "The success we had in getting him out the last two games was due more to outstanding stuff by Steve Carlton and Tug McGraw than any particular way they were trying to pitch him. They threw him some pitches that were unhittable."

Brett doubts if he'll ever threaten .400 again. "I don't think I can hit four hundred," he says. "To hit four hundred, a guy's going to have to get more leg hits than I normally get. I had a taste of it and hitting over four hundred is an unbelievable feeling."

Willie Wilson

When Willie Wilson whirled through his senior year at Summit High School in New Jersey, major league baseball was on the outside looking in. College football recruiters were lined up around the block. Wilson, a 6-foot 3-inch running back and track star whose speed was edging toward world class, seemed destined to play four years of big time

Above: *George Brett of the Kansas City Royals has a lot to smile about. In 1980 he hit .390, collected 175 hits in 117 games, including 24 home runs and 118 runs batted in.* Opposite: *Willie Wilson, outfielder for the Royals, has blazing speed and the ability to get on base. He hit for a .326 average and stole 79 bases in 1980. In the next decade he may bat .350 and top Lou Brock's season high of 118 stolen bases.*

college football and graduate into the NFL ranks.

The kid was a brilliant baseball prospect, too, a whippet-quick outfielder who ran the bases with drag-racer speed. Major league scouts flocked to Summit, but most of them felt they were dealing with another Condredge Holloway. Holloway was a superb all-around athlete from Huntsville, Alabama, with the potential to be a great major league shortstop. On the day of the June free agent draft, members of the University of Tennessee football coaching staff "babysat" Holloway in a Florida motel room to make sure he didn't change his mind and tell the Montreal Expos, who would have made him the first selection in the draft, that he had changed his mind. Holloway had a fine career as a running quarterback at Tennessee, but the years of football training robbed him of the range and suppleness a shortstop needs. He wound up having a mediocre career in the Canadian Football League.

Wilson seemed determined to play college football and the University of Maryland had the inside track. Most baseball scouts advised their organizations that Wilson was not worth the waste of a high draft choice. But the Kansas City Royals hung tough. In the end, economics won. The Royals told Wilson they would give him a $90,000 bonus to sign.

"It was a difficult decision," baseball's most devastating base runner says. "Football was the big sport in our town.

"I wasn't in a ghetto situation, or anything like that. But we could use the money then. It was a tough decision then, but it turned out to be the right one."

On the day of the June 1974 draft, the Royals were understandably nervous. They knew Maryland coach Jerry Claiborne wouldn't give Wilson up without a battle. "The day of the draft a number of scouts, general managers, and directors of minor league operations came by our table to say that we'd never sign him, that he'd play football," a Royals official says. "Some of them told us they'd talked to Willie the day before the draft and that he'd sworn he was going to play football. There's a lot of excuses around the league these days on the Wilson signing, but the fact of the matter is that we did our homework better than they did."

Willie did not take the minor leagues by storm. He had so much trouble against righthanders that the Royals turned him into a switch-hitter. But during the 1980 season, Wilson became one of baseball's most explosive offensive stars. He joined Cardinals star Garry Templeton as one of two switch-

hitters in history to collect 100 or more hits from each side of the plate in a single season. Running with abandon, Wilson batted .325, led the majors with 230 hits and 133 runs scored, and stole 79 bases.

"The only base runner I've ever seen who matched him going from first to third was Willie Davis," said Twins manager Gene Mauch. "Any time the ball bounces in the infield twice he's going to be on base."

Just 26 going into the 1981 season, Wilson was still a raw talent with room for improvement in what is already a dazzling offensive repertoire.

"He's still learning the pitchers," says Royals manager Jim Frey. "He just outruns the ball right now. Once he learns to exploit pitchers' weaknesses the sky's the limit. I think once he starts stealing bases on a combination of speed and technique that he can steal one hundred twenty-five bases a year, easy."

Wilson led the American League with 83 steals in 1979 and his two-season total of 162 is the best back-to-back performance by a big league player since 1915–16, when the great Ty Cobb totaled 164. During one 1980 stretch, Willie stole 32 consecutive bases without being thrown out, an American League record.

His splendid season ended on a sour note, though. Willie was a futile batsman during the Royals' World Series loss to the Phillies. He struck out 12 times, a Series record. "We felt the key to stopping them offensively was keeping Wilson and U.L. Washington off base," said Phillies manager Dallas Green. "We knew George Brett and their other big hitters would get their hits, but we didn't want Wilson and Washington raising hell on the bases. Keeping them in the dugout proved to be the key."

Frey feels Wilson has the potential to hit .350.

"Hell," Gene Mauch snaps, "Willie Wilson might be able to run three-fifty."

Fred Lynn

The anthracite regions of Pennsylvania have produced a seemingly endless supply of tough, burly football linemen. The schoolyards of Washington, D.C., have kept the NBA supplied with stars at the Elgin Baylor, Adrian Dantley level. But if you want baseball players, California is the mother lode. Just one high school in Oakland, the famed McClymonds High, has turned out Curt Flood, Vada Pinson, and Willie Stargell.

"No doubt about it," says Phillies general manager Paul Owens, who started in the player development phase of the game as a scout operating out of the Bakersfield area, "there are more major league prospects in California alone in an average year than the rest of the states combined. And that's at all levels—high school, junior college, and major college. Some years, Southern Cal's program is the equivalent of a Triple A ballclub."

Fred Lynn is a prototype model of the kind of athlete California has been producing for baseball. Lynn could have signed for a hefty bonus out of high school, but was recruited for Southern Cal's high-powered program. He had an all-American career and was signed for $40,000 by the Red Sox in 1973. His minor league career was brief and relatively undistinguished, but he burst loudly onto the Fenway Park scene with one of the greatest rookie seasons in baseball history. Average? Lynn hit .331. Power? He led the American League with 49 doubles, drove in 105 runs, and powered 21 homers, despite the hostile dimensions of Fenway for lefthanded hitters. Lynn was a unanimous choice for Rookie of the Year and led the Red Sox to the pennant.

Nagging injuries kept him from repeating his debut, MVP performance until 1979, when he won the batting title with a .333 average, punctuating it with 39 homers and 122 RBI. And, injuries slowed him again in 1980, when he appeared in just 110 games. Fred made more news on the financial pages than the sports pages.

When healthy, Lynn is obviously one of the game's premier talents, an athlete gifted in every phase. But his medical history suggests that the team that has agreed to his asking price assumes a high degree of risk. That risk has been taken because he's the kind of dominator who can turn a franchise around.

Baseball people still speak in awed tones of the June night in 1975 when he had the biggest game of his career. When the mushroom-shaped cloud over Detroit's Tiger Stadium dissipated, Lynn had flogged five hits, three of them homers, and driven in 10 runs, the top offensive performance by a rookie in baseball history.

Lynn became involved in a fascinating round of negotiations during the early winter of 1980 and 1981. Cognizant of his long-standing desire to play with a California contender, the Red Sox tried to engineer a trade for their star.

The Boston management knew it had almost no chance to re-sign Lynn, who was going into the option year of his contract. Club president Haywood Sullivan tried frantically to engineer a trade with a club which would be willing to meet Lynn's salary demands while sending Boston some players to help offset the loss of his centerfielder.

After a long round of negotiations, Sullivan appeared to have worked out a trade with Los Angeles vice-president Al Campanis which would have sent Lynn to the Dodgers for a package of youngsters, including 1980 Rookie of the Year Steve Howe, a lefthanded reliever, and swift outfielder Rudy Law. But that face-saving transaction fell apart when Lynn told the Dodgers through agent Jerry Kapstein that he would not sign more than a one-year contract if traded. Fred was determined to wield the mighty hammer of free agency, confident that he could easily command more in an open market than world record holder Winfield.

The Dodgers were in shock. They had offered Lynn a five-year, $5 million contract which would have made him the highest paid player in the history of the franchise. "We didn't feel it was good business to give up three or four outstanding prospects for a player we had a chance to lose to the highest bidder next season," Campanis said.

Sullivan even turned to Boston's hated rival, the Yankees, for a possible trade. George Steinbrenner seemed willing to give up ace lefthander Ron Guidry for Lynn. But even a man as lavish with money as the New York impresario was unwilling to stick his neck into the one-year option noose. Lynn seemed destined to spend one more summer in Fenway Park before becoming the highest paid player in baseball history.

The Red Sox wriggled out of what was turning into a blind alley following a horrendous clerical oversight which could have resulted in Lynn being declared a free agent *before* the 1981 season. It seems his 1981 contract had been mailed 24 hours after the deadline and the Players Association took the Red Sox to arbitration.

Just hours before what could have been an unfavorable ruling, the Boston club sent their star to the California Angels in a multi-player trade which brought them veteran outfielder Joe Rudi as Lynn's replacement. Lynn, in California at last, immediately signed a four-year contract believed to call for a salary of $1.4 million a year.

The Sun Belt had won again.

Mike Schmidt

Mike Schmidt owes it all to a pair of battered sneakers. The Phillies' brilliant, home run hitting third baseman was climbing a tree in the backyard of his parents' home in Dayton, where the Schmidts operated a swimming club. Mike was nine years old on the day he climbed higher in the tree than he had ever climbed before and reached a little higher into its thick tangle of branches.

Years of slow growth had concealed a high tension power line which ran through the top of the tree. When Schmidt reached out to establish a hand-hold on it, he thought it was just another leafy branch. The cable sent a lethal jolt of 20,000 volts surging through his body.

"My sneaks saved my life," Schmidt recalls. "At least that's what they told me at the hospital when I came to." Mike raised his left pants leg and displayed a round scar the size of a fifty cent piece. "The rubber soles of the sneaks grounded me. The electric current had no place to go when it reached a non-conducter like rubber. It backed up and exited through the path of least resistance, which happened to be the thin layer of flesh over my shin. It happened so fast I was blasted out of the tree before I received enough juice to kill me. If I had been wearing leather soles I would have been one big conducter and I would have been killed almost instantly. As it was, the doctors say it was close to being a miracle."

Schmidt survived to become a great all-around athlete in high school and at Ohio University. Like Pittsburgh's Dave Parker, Mike seemed headed toward a football career until knee injuries turned him toward baseball.

People who watched him play during his amateur days say he could have been an NFL strong safety or an NBA backcourt man. But when Phillies midwest scout Tony Lucadello joined the hunt, Schmidt was playing shortstop for the Ohio University Bobcats.

"What I saw first was a future home run hitter," Lucadello says. "He had great wrists and a natural power stroke. He was playing short at about a hundred ninety pounds and I knew he'd get bigger. He had great range and an average arm, but in my scouting reports I projected him as a third baseman."

Schmidt was coming off surgery on both knees when Lucadello scouted him and he had a sore right shoulder which inhibited his throwing. By the time he arrived in Philadelphia in 1972, Mike's speed and throwing arm were both well above major league average.

But his rookie year was a nightmare. His at

bats were either boom or bust and there were far more days of bust than boom. In a 132-game debut as the Phillies' regular third baseman, Schmidt batted a sickly .196, lowest of any major league regular. Part of his batting failures could be attributed to a shoulder injury he suffered diving for a ball toward the close of spring training. The rest was due to anxiety, inexperience, and a burning desire to achieve instant stardom. But he showed flashes of raw power, punctuating his 136 strikeouts with 18 homers.

"One of the things I'm proudest of during my seven seasons managing in Philadelphia is the patience I showed with Mike Schmidt," says former manager Danny Ozark. "I don't think many managers would have stuck with him as long as I did. But we weren't going anywhere. My job was to build a team for the future and the future was built around the Mike Schmidts."

The reign of terror began in Schmidt's sophomore season, when he led the majors with 36 homers, an act he repeated the next two years, when he hit 38. A series of injuries cut his power totals to 21 homers and 78 RBI in 1978, but he bounced back in 1979 with his finest power season—45 homers and a league-leading 120 RBI.

But Schmidt, a home run king, a four-time Gold Glove winner at his position, still had one more mountain to climb. He had to live down a reputation as a man who dotted his career with meaningless homers, who rarely delivered in clutch situations. Baseball men pointed to his .182 average in 11 homerless playoff games as proof of that widespread indictment.

It all came together for Schmidt during his superb 1980 season. Avoiding major power slumps for all but a three-week stretch in August, Schmidt led the Phillies to their first World Series title in 98 years. He led the majors with 48 homers. More important to the National League's MVP, Schmidt put the Phillies over the top with an incredible string of key homers in the final week, including the two-run shot in Montreal which clinched the Eastern Division title on the next to last day of the season. His two-homer, seven-RBI performance against Kansas City earned him the World Series MVP award.

"This was the season when the Phillies and Mike Schmidt chased away a lot of ghosts," he said. "I've proved to the fans and to myself that I have the ability to perform at a championship level with the money on the line. I feel like I've climbed the last mountain. And the view is unbelievable."

Opposite: *Mike Schmidt, third baseman for the Philadelphia Phillies, shows the concentration and arm extension that are the marks of a big league power hitter. In 1979 he was the league leader with 120 RBI.*
Above: *Dave Winfield, San Diego free agent picked up in 1981 by the Yankees for a multimillion-dollar contract. When he graduated from college, the 6'6", 220-pound athlete was drafted by professional football and basketball teams as well as by the San Diego Padres.*

Dave Winfield

The powerful 6-foot 6-inch, 220-pound frame of Dave Winfield first achieved a high degree of national visibility during a college basketball game between Wisconsin and Ohio State. A fight broke out between the bitter Big Ten rivals and Winfield, a power forward for Wisconsin, was right in the middle of it, tossing Buckeye players around like rag dolls.

By the time Winfield graduated in June 1973, he had been drafted by no fewer than four professional teams representing three major sports. Although he hadn't played football since his high school days in St. Paul, the Minnesota Vikings drafted him as a tight end. The NBA Atlanta Hawks and ABA Utah Stars drafted him as a power forward. And the San Diego Padres chose him in the first round of the June baseball draft.

Winfield signed with the Padres for a $100,000 bonus. San Diego was a shabby expansion team in 1973, mired in last place each of its four years of existence. Attendance was woeful, the owner, C. Arnholt Smith, was embroiled in a financing scandal involving 1972 Nixon campaign funds, and the team was on the verge of moving to Washington, D.C. The Padres, hungry for a young star, immediately installed Winfield in the outfield without an inning of minor league experience. That was probably a mistake. The Padres realized Winfield was in over his head and used him sparingly the remainder of his rookie season.

Since then, Dave has been a fine player, a solid average and RBI man. But after eight full seasons, his offensive statistics are below the superstar plateau. Only in 1979 could his performance be termed devastating. He hit .308 with 34 homers and a league-leading 118 RBI. Considering the canyonesque dimensions of Jack Murphy Stadium, those were excellent achievements indeed.

But the real Dave Winfield Story emerged from the world of high finance, a variation of the Horatio Alger theme which would see him go from affluence to grandeur. And to understand the entry of Winfield into the 1980 free agent market and its spinoff effect on the economics of the entire game is to understand the new financial realities facing baseball.

Efforts by the Padres to sign Winfield to a new long-term contract during the 1980 season ended in bitterness and name-calling. Management charged that the Winfield Foundation, a charitable endeavor or funded by Dave to aid youth, was nothing more than a self-serving tax writeoff which was actually provided, interest-free, by the ballclub. His impending free agency was the most awaited event of the off-season. Before the November reentry draft, Winfield sent letters to a number of "have-not" clubs, advising them not to waste a selection on him. This outraged several baseball men, including lame duck White Sox president, Bill Veeck. After the draft, Winfield narrowed his choices to three teams: the Yankees, thought to have a lock on him throughout the proceedings, Ted Turner's Atlanta Braves, and the New York Mets. The Yankees and Mets attendance war drove the ante up and up.

Winfield was eventually unveiled by George Steinbrenner at a media circus. His 10-year contract called for a "minimum" of $1.5 million a year. Through a cost-of-living clause in the complicated contract, which was surely beefed up by paid life insurance policies and interest-free loans, it was calculated he could earn as much as $23.3 million during its life, a figure that would make him history's highest paid athlete by far.

In January 1981, the Yankees and Winfield's agent, Al Frohman, released a statement adjusting the contract's terms.

It turned out Steinbrenner wasn't keeping pace with the spiraling cost-of-living index when the original deal was verbalized. The *New York Times* reported that the Yankee owner thought the original deal was worth $7 million less than the reported $23.3 million and was so upset when he learned the true figures he threatened to call off the deal.

The original contract called for a maximum 10 percent raise each year based on the projected rise in the cost of living. That would hike his salary from $1.3 million the first year to $3.3 million the tenth, assuming a modest 10 percent rise in the inflation. When the lawyers tucked away their pocket calculators, Winfield is believed to have settled for an adjusted possible total of between $19.3 million and $20.3 million. Dave will not be eligible for the food stamps program.

The question that was immediately raised, of course, was the impact the Winfield contract would have on a salary structure which had already pushed the average annual wage to $175,000 for 650 big league players. If a good player with less than superstar credentials is worth $1.5 million or more a year, what will the legitimate superstars like Mike Schmidt, George Brett, Garry Templeton, and Fred Lynn be worth? The mind boggles.

(Lynn, who was traded by Boston to the California Angels in January 1981, signed a four-year contract believed to be worth about $1.4 million a year.)

Amateur economists figure that to justify his vast salary, Winfield will have to average .450, hit 85 homers, and drive in 215 runs. If he achieves even half of those totals, Dave Winfield will be considered the bargain of a nutty decade.

Dave Parker

There is one moment in every catcher's career when it is almost guaranteed that his life will flash before his eyes. That moment will come when Pittsburgh outfielder Dave Parker is thundering down the third base line in full gallop, the catcher is braced to block the plate, and the throw is coming from right field, his blind side.

The collision will be awesome, a 250-pound man with sprinter's speed crashing into a stationary 195-pound catcher. "All you can do is brace yourself and try not to let him get you too solid," says former Phillies catcher Johnny Oates, who once spent 10 weeks on the disabled list after a collision with Parker. "When he's coming down the line you can feel the ground shake."

Parker should wear a row of catcher's mitt decals on his helmet, the way World War II flyers painted enemy kills under their cockpits. Besides Oates, Parker also has disabled the Mets' John Stearns. But there is nothing dirty or illegal about his catcher-burying style. In fact, he came away from two collisions with disabling injuries himself—a shoulder injury and a broken cheekbone.

Like Dave Winfield, Parker is a graphic illustration of what happens when a great all-around athlete chooses baseball over football or basketball. Parker could have attended the college of his choice on his football or basketball prowess. But knee injuries made him reassess his future and when the Pirates selected him in the fourteenth round of the June 1970 draft, Parker signed for a very modest bonus. Unlike Winfield, who jumped from the college campus to the majors, Parker started at rock bottom and spent most of four seasons learning his trade in the minors.

In a sport where big rarely means good, Parker is probably the best all-around big man to play an everyday position.

At 6 feet 7 inches and 275 pounds, former Los Angeles slugger Frank Howard had great home run power, but he struck out a lot and was a liability in the field. Parker, however, has won two National League batting titles, an MVP award, and a Gold Glove. He has a Howitzer throwing arm, great range in the field, and speed enough to be a stolen base threat.

There is a chink in Parker's armor, though, one which cast a small but discernible shadow on his fine career. Dave has never developed into the awesome home run hitter one would expect a man with his size and power to be, a masher in the 40–50 range.

"I think of him as a power hitter rather than a home run hitter," Pete Rose says. "Even though I don't hit more than a couple of homers a year, I feel I'm also a power hitter. Dave's basically a line drive hitter who waits a long time on the ball. He stings the ball through the alleys. If he was a pull hitter, he'd probably lose twenty-five points off his average and hit his forty to forty-five homers. He's probably more dangerous hitting three-twenty and twenty-five homers. He doesn't drive in a hundred runs every year because he's never had a three-hundred hitter or a guy who walks a lot in front of him. Check your big RBI guys; they always have a three-hundred hitter or high walk guy in front of them. Dave's the ideal number-three hitter. Don't forget, he's always had Willie Stargell hitting cleanup behind him, so he's up there to hit a single or double and let Willie drive him in."

Parker played the 1980 season with a variety of injuries, including a knee so bad it required postseason surgery. His average tailed off to .295, he hit only 17 homers, and drove in just 79 runs. That would be considered an above-average season for most outfielders. But Parker was earning $900,000 a year to perform in a blue collar town where the majority of the fans punch a clock and work at hard jobs in the steel mills.

Parker received daily hate mail and was pelted by dangerous objects thrown from the bleachers on several occasions. The experience left him with a bitter taste. He was one of several players to discover in 1980 that a big man who makes a big salary also creates big expectations.

It doesn't help Parker's image in the Steel City that he is baseball's version of Muhammad Ali, so outspoken he makes Reggie Jackson sound like Mr. Humble.

He runs the Pirates' boisterous clubhouse with the bluster of a Marine drill instructor. His teammates, a loose, uncomplicated group, tolerate his chest-thumping antics and macho patter with good humor. They hurl Dave's mock anger and insults right back at him.

Opposite: *Jim Rice, a powerhouse for the Red Sox, hit .302 with 22 homers and 102 RBI as a rookie in 1975.*
Above: *That same year, rookie teammate Fred Lynn, now with the Angels, hit .331 with 21 homers and 105 RBI.*

99

"I'm a legend," Parker will announce to the clubhouse at large.

"You're a legend all right," infielder Phil Garner hollers. "They're talking about how you *used* to be."

Another day, outfielder Lee Lacy was expounding philosophically about the hero-one-day, bum-the-next nature of the game. "The game is full of peaks and valleys, peaks and valleys," Lacy said.

Parker reacted predictably. "I've only had peaks," he said, "no valleys. Maybe I hit a couple of potholes, but no valleys. I'm everything they say I am."

But away from his peers, Parker can be serious and introspective.

"Best player in the game?" he mused. "Just another title they put on my head. Frankly, I think there's a lot of excellent talent in baseball. I just happened to be a guy that kind of represents every feature of the game—my offensive ability, my defensive ability, my leadership, the way I run the bases . . ."

Unfortunately, at 6 feet 5 inches and 250 pounds people will always demand a little more.

Jim Rice

Fenway Park, the rococo Boston monument to a bygone baseball age, is a paradise for a righthanded power hitter. The fence in left, dubbed the "Green Monster," by American League pitchers, looks close enough to touch. Any ball hit decently in the air to left has a chance to sail over it or bounce off it for extra bases.

Unfortunately, either through design or organizational ineptitude, Boston's most famed power hitters over the years have usually been lefthanded—Ted Williams, Carl Yastrzemski, and Fred Lynn, to name some prominent ones.

Which brings us to Jim Rice, the powerful outfielder-designated hitter who had the bad luck to be a Sox rookie in 1975. All the powerful kid from Anderson, South Carolina, did was hit .302, slam 22 homers, and drive in 102 runs. And all that got him was the runner-up position in Rookie of the Year voting. The winner, of course, was yearling teammate Lynn, who won the batting title, the MVP and Rookie of the Year awards, and most of the headlines in Boston's notoriously competitive newspapers.

Add to that the Red Sox reputation for racism—they were among the last major league teams to sign black players and have been accused of tokenism—and the ingredients were all there for controversy involving Rice.

There was plenty of controversy when Rice charged in a *Sport* magazine story before the 1978 season that Lynn was moved through the minors faster than he was because the Boston front office was more partial to white stars.

The most damaging quote was this: "Race has to be a factor when Fred Lynn can hit two-forty in the minors and I can hit three-forty, and he gets a starting job before I do."

The town's baseball writers and columnists tore into the story like sharks attacking a bleeding swimmer. Rice backed off his published position, charging he was misquoted and that the Red Sox had been nothing but fair to him. Rice also stopped talking to reporters altogether.

His silence was an eloquent one, though. Until a foot injury slowed him in July, Jim was attacking the Green Monster and other more distant fences around the league at a record pace. He finished the season with a .315 average, 46 homers, and 139 RBI. It was a season when Yankee lefthander Ron Guidry was so overpowering that many felt he would win both the MVP and Cy Young awards. Rice also predicted as much. Speaking to writers again when it suited him, he said he heard a lot of talk that the press would vote him MVP only if the Red Sox won the pennant, other whispers that he wouldn't win it because of his press boycott.

His fears were unfounded, of course. Rice was the runaway MVP winner.

He was playing golf in Las Vegas the day the award was announced. Dozens of writers who called for interviews learned that he was not waiting by the phone to hear of his canonization. One of the first writers to reach him when he finished his round was Martin Ralbovsky, who asked how he felt about winning.

"I just got back from shooting a seventy-nine," Jim said. "That's more important."

The next season, Rice signed a long-term $5 million contract after long and bitter negotiations. But he did not suffer from an MVP or Long Contract slump. In some respects, his .325, 39 homer, 130 RBI season was just as impressive as his MVP performance. The Red Sox had an unbelievable string of injuries and Rice and Lynn were forced to carry almost the entire offensive load.

In 1980, it was Rice's turn to join Don Zimmer's casualties. He missed 38 games, but still managed to hit a decent 24 homers with 86 RBI.

With Lynn gone to California in an early 1981

trade and Carl Yastrzemski almost eligible for Medicare benefits, Rice should have the spotlight to himself until the Red Sox can rebuild what was once an awesome offensive lineup. Just 28, Jim should be a dominant slugger until the end of the decade.

Garry Templeton

If a Hollywood producer was casting for a baseball movie, he wouldn't pick Lou Ferrigno to play the shortstop. A Mickey Rooney type would do, a scrawny, feisty guy who couldn't hack his way out of a wet paper sack with a machete.

That's the popular image of the major league shortstop. If you drew a composite of all the shortstops to play in the big leagues over the years, the result would be an athlete under six feet who weighs less than 165. He would have cat-quick reflexes, excellent range, and a strong throwing arm. He would be a hitter in the .250 to .275 range and each time he hit a home run, somebody in the dugout would lapse into a mock faint.

It is very difficult to win a baseball championship without a gifted defensive shortstop. He is in the middle of the infield action, a guy who will handle more chances during the course of a season than anybody but the first baseman. His ability to turn the double play will be a key factor in whether a team gets out of jams with men on base or succumbs to big innings.

So when a major league team shops for a shortstop, defense is always the highest priority. And that's why a shortstop whose offensive ability matches his glovework is one of the game's most rare and desirable commodities. The best all-around shortstop of the 1970s was the Reds' David Concepcion, a Venezuelan with no weakness in the field and enough extra base power to often bat third against lefthanded pitchers. Concepcion, in addition to being a Gold Glover, was also a run-producer, a man consistently near the top of the Reds' stats when runs scored and runs batted in were combined.

A lanky, powerful kid named Garry Templeton burst into the St. Louis Cardinals' lineup on a regular basis in 1977.

His raw ability was dazzling. Templeton had a sprinter's speed and an arm like a rightfielder. He had the additional advantage of being a switch-hitter. The son of former Negro League infielder Spavia Templeton was raw as a winter morning in Buffalo, though. His powerful arm was so erratic

that customers in the box seats behind first base should have been issued riot helmets. In his first four full seasons with the Cardinals, Templeton averaged nearly 40 errors. But his range was so startling that he reached balls routinely that normal shortstops would automatically chalk up as base hits.

What set him apart from the rest of the world's shortstops was his offense. In his first full season, Garry cracked 200 hits, a goal most shortstops never achieve in a lifetime of trying. He batted .322 and led the National League with a startling 18 triples.

Templeton, unhappy with his contract and suffering a natural letdown as pitchers probed for chinks in his offensive armor, fell off to .280 in 1978. In 1979, Templeton bounced back and achieved what no switch-hitter had achieved before him—not even Pete Rose or the great Mickey Mantle. On the way to a league-leading 211 hits, Garry became the first switch-hitter in major league history to accumulate 100 or more hits from each side of the plate. (Okay, he had to cheat a little, batting righthanded against a righthanded pitcher to collect his one-hundredth hit from that side. But the record still counts.)

Baseball people spend a lot of idle time asking hypothetical questions. One of their favorites is, "If you had to start a club from scratch and had your choice of any big league player, which one would you pick first?"

Templeton's name is dropped often, a shortstop you could build a franchise around.

During the 1980 season, the Cardinals, picked by many experts to win or at least seriously contend for a division title, became a monumental flop. The same experts blamed much of their tumble to fourth place on an inadequate pitching staff. But the more astute also pointed to an injury which kept Templeton out of 45 games. He still managed to hit .319 and collect 161 hits, a better than average total for a shortstop who appeared in all 162 games.

Templeton has been involved in his share of controversy, which seems to be a prerequisite for stardom in the eighties. Balloting for the annual All-Star Game is in the hands of the fans and the teams in recent years have been dominated by fans in cities whose teams have the largest attendance. In 1979, Templeton, having by far the best season of any National League shortstop, was buried by an avalanche of votes for the Reds' Concepcion and the Phillies' defensive genius Larry Bowa. When

Opposite: *The Pittsburgh Pirates' big man, Dave Parker, can do it all, as his two National League batting titles, MVP award, and Gold Glove attest. He also has one of the best throwing arms of any outfielder in the game, and can use his football abilities to break up plays on the bases.* Above: *Gary Carter, brilliant young catcher for the Montreal Expos, has authentic home-run power and is considered the best catcher in the game since Johnny Bench. In 1980 Carter was runner-up for MVP with 29 homers and 101 runs batted in.*

Templeton was selected to the team as a reserve by National League manager Tommy Lasorda, he uttered the famous words, "If I ain't startin', I ain't departin'." Templeton stayed home.

The voting produced an even greater travesty in 1980. Templeton, leading the league with 102 hits at the time of the final vote tally, was trounced by Bill Russell, thanks to massive ballot-box stuffing in Dodger Stadium.

Once more, Templeton declined to serve as a reserve. For the second straight season, baseball's best all-around shortstop at age 25, went fishing.

Gary Carter

Dick Williams knows the agony of losing a star player in the crucible of a pennant stretch drive. The Montreal manager remembered the year he was leading the Oakland A's and star outfielder Reggie Jackson tore up a knee in the final week of the regular season and watched the playoffs and World Series on crutches.

"That was tough," Williams said on a late September evening in 1979, "but the A's were an experienced championship club. We missed Reggie, but the guys stepped in to take up the slack. Losing Garry Carter at this stage of the thing is a helluva lot tougher."

And it was. Carter, the Expos' brilliant young catcher, ended his season in a home plate collision with Alberto Lois during a key victory over the Pirates, the team Montreal was duelling down the stretch. The Expos lost the Eastern Division title on the final day of the season when Phillies ace Steve Carlton shut them out 2–0 with Carter watching.

Carter wanted to play despite a painful thumb injury which made it almost impossible for him to grip a bat. He tried to take batting practice and, afterward, the team physician told him he would need immediate surgery if he didn't want to jeopardize his skyrocketing career.

Gary is that rare catcher who comes along once every decade or so—Johnny Bench was the last—who combines home run hitting power, the ability to hit for decent average, and remarkable defensive prowess, including expert handling of a young pitching staff. Once a team has a catcher like a Bench or a Carter it is spoiled for life. He becomes the cornerstone of the franchise.

In 1980, the Expos lost the division title once again on the next to last day, falling to the eventual World Champion Phillies. Carter had another splendid season. The all-star catcher slammed 29 homers and drove in 101 runs to finish second to the Phils' Mike Schmidt in the MVP balloting. At 27, his best years seemed to be ahead of him.

The Expos made the 6-foot 2-inch, 205-pound Californian their number-three draft choice in June 1972. He spent three years in the minors learning his difficult trade.

Carter caught on with the ebullient Expos fans immediately. He runs to first at a sprint à la Pete Rose and plays the game with a contagious enthusiasm.

"We feel he's the best catcher in the game right now and should be for years to come," says Montreal special assignment scout Charlie Fox. "He's about as close to the young Johnny Bench as you could possibly get. I still don't think he's reached his full power potential. He could easily be a forty-plus home run man."

Duke Snider, a Hall of Famer who now broadcasts for the Expos, played with the great Roy Campanella in Brooklyn. He sees a future Hall of Famer in Carter. "I'm even more impressed with his catching than with his hitting," Snider says. "It's hard to measure his value behind the plate. He does so much with the pitchers."

Carter credits his emergence as a great catcher to the abandonment of an ill-advised 1974 experiment, when the Expos called him up at the end of the season and stuck him in right field.

"I was out of position," he says. "I was running into walls and hurting myself. When Charlie Fox took over at the end of 1976, I began to play regular catcher and things fell into place."

In one of the game's small ironies, the catcher responsible for Carter's abortive presence in right field was former number-one draft choice Barry Foote. Foote is a journeyman for the Chicago Cubs.

"He was the second best catcher in baseball, now he's the best," says Pirates manager Chuck Tanner.

When he's blocking the plate or running to it, Gary asks no quarter and gives none, as Mets catcher John Stearns, a former all-Big Eight defensive back, discovered in 1979. Carter bowled Stearns over at the plate and the Mets' catcher came up swinging. There was a wild, bench-clearing free-for-all and both players were ejected.

"I'm not out there to hurt anybody," Carter said. "I'm just trying to play good, hard baseball."

Gary Carter plays good baseball. He plays hard baseball. Which is why he will remain the premier catcher of the 1980s.

104

Gary Carter, who just turned 27 at the beginning of the 1981 season, plays the game with skill and toughness. He gets the most from his pitchers, blocks the plate fearlessly, and hits with consistency and power.

Above: *Garry Templeton, shortstop for the St. Louis Cardinals, has great speed and range and a rifle throwing arm. In 1979 he had a hundred or more hits from each side of the plate, and hit .319 in 1980.* Opposite: *Paul Molitor of the Milwaukee Brewers is one of the most talented and versatile players in the game.*

Above: *Garry Templeton, in his first full season in
1977, batted .322 with 200 hits, including 18 triples.*
Opposite: *Paul Molitor hit .322 in 1979 while playing second and short. He can also play center field.*

Paul Molitor

To select Paul Molitor, the Milwaukee Brewers' brilliant young talent, as one of the 10 players who will dominate baseball in the 1980s, is probably to do a disservice to his infield running mate Robin Yount, whom Boston *Globe* baseball expert Peter Gammons calls, "an underrated young superstar."

Such is the price of playing big league shortstop at the tender age of 19. At 25, Yount, the American League's best all-around shortstop, was already a six-year veteran when the 1981 season began. Robin was already an established star when the Brewers plucked Molitor from the University of Minnesota campus as their number-one draft choice in 1977.

Molitor played one season in the minors and was the American League Rookie of the Year in 1978, playing second, short when Yount was injured or resting, and third. He broke through to stardom in 1979, ranking among the league leaders with a .322 average for a team of dock wallopers who led the league in homers. Once more, Molitor played both short and second base.

Paul's versatility is so impressive that the Brewers ordered him to report for 1981 spring training prepared to play centerfield in the wake of a flurry of off-season trades. That was fine with the all-star second baseman. "I'm very comfortable in the outfield," he said. "Actually, I was an outfielder most of the time in high school and college."

His decision to attend college probably saved him years of kicking around in the low minor leagues. The Cardinals drafted him on the twenty-eighth round his senior year, but he didn't sign.

Molitor underlines another trend in modern baseball. More and more teams are teaching their young players to play more than one position.

"The day when you sign by position is just about over with the exception of pitchers," one big league farm director says. "The trend will be to draft the best athlete available no matter what his position and then try to teach him to play a position where there will be a future need at the big league level. Instruction at the minor league level is better than it's ever been and we find that the better athlete is very adaptable if you get him early enough in his career. You can't teach running speed, but we find that the player who can run and throw has a lot of options available."

Keith Moreland, the Phillies' catching prospect, carries so many gloves out to a workout he can barely handle them all. He works out daily behind the plate, at first and third base, and in the outfield.

"I'm playing behind an all-star quality catcher [Bob Boone] and I know he has the job," Moreland says. "So if I want to get in the amount of playing time I need at this stage of my career I have to be able to fill in wherever they need me. The idea is, you can't get more than one at bat a game in the National League if you can't play more than one position."

Even an established young star like Molitor is taking all his gloves to spring training. "I'll probably play a lot of outfield in 1981," he said. "But I know I'm a pretty good infielder and they know it. If Robin gets hurt or somebody else doesn't work out at second, I'll probably be right back in there."

Meanwhile, his gifted contemporary, Yount, has shown signs of developing into the game's foremost power-hitting shortstop. Until last season, Yount had never hit more than nine homers in one year. But Robin increased his strength in off-season workouts and 1980 pitchers discovered a mouse that roared. Yount slammed 23 homers, drove in 87 runs, and stole 20 bases to prove he hadn't lost his speed.

It seems almost criminal to break up a double play combination—Molitor and Yount—capable of piling up that kind of offense.

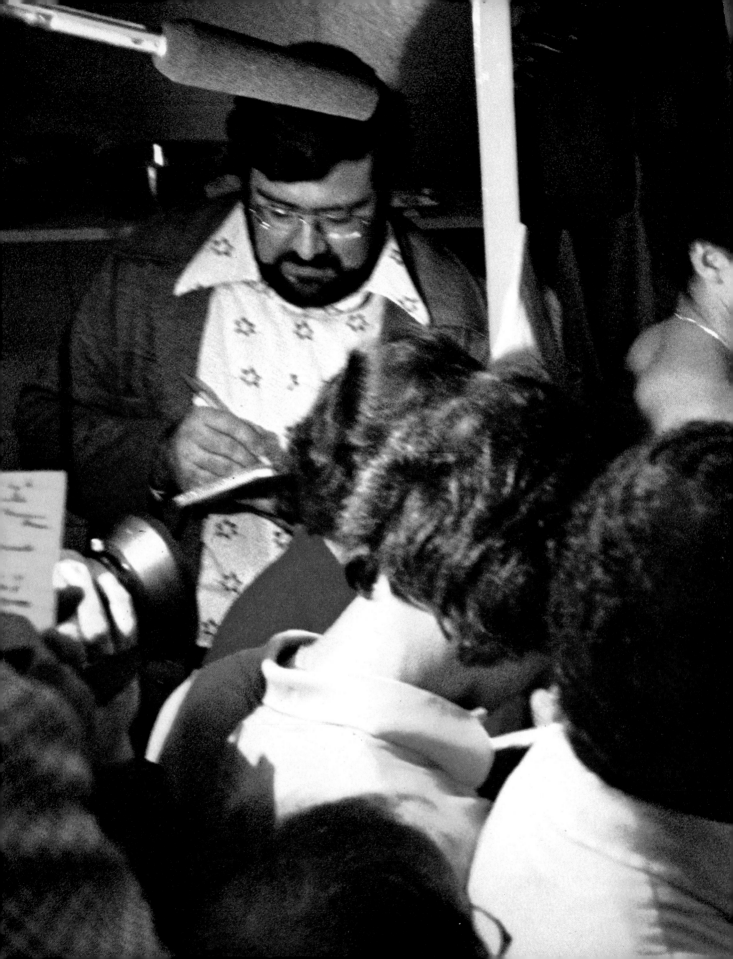

7

Us Against Them

"A baseball writer's relationship with a ballplayer is a cop-and-crook relationship. You're not there as his buddy, as his fan, as his teammate. It's an adversary relationship. A lot of writers think that ballplayers love them. But ballplayers are amused by writers and consider them necessary evils. One thing I know about ballplayers: They never thank you for the praise. But they really complain if you rip them. They think they are entitled to good notices."

—Jimmy Cannon

Larry Eichel was a sensitive young man in his late twenties, a Harvard graduate. As a cityside reporter for the Philadelphia *Inquirer,* Eichel was a member of a news team that won a 1972 Pulitzer prize for its superb coverage of the devastation wrought on northeastern Pennsylvania by Hurricane Agnes.

Eichel was raised in Cincinnati, a devout Reds fan. He had a brilliant newspaper future—Larry is currently chief of the *Inquirer*'s West Coast Bureau—but he wanted to give baseball writing a try. The beat opened up when Bruce Keidan was made a bureau chief in western Pennsylvania. Eichel volunteered.

All the glamour, all the delicious expectations, all the preconceived notions Larry Eichel harbored concerning what it would be like to cover a major league baseball team as a traveling writer were shattered before the roses were in bloom. Eichel wrote with precision and candor. He was quick and accurate. He covered his rookie's knowledge of some of the game's strategic intricacies by asking questions, doing his homework.

For his pains, Eichel was called a "hippie Jew" behind his back, a "bearded creep" to his face.

In an ugly incident on a team bus outside the Montreal Airport after the Phillies had lost a Sunday afternoon game to the Expos, Eichel was verbally savaged by shortstop Larry Bowa. Eichel sat there and took it with as much dignity as he could muster under the grim circumstances. But he didn't have to take it forever. He was too bright and too qualified for other areas of his profession to prostrate his sensibilities. Larry Eichel finished the season. Among first-year baseball writers in America, he was the runaway rookie of the year. But he asked for another assignment. Not yet 30 years old, Larry Eichel was an ex-baseball writer.

It's a jungle out there.

After the 1978 season, the Philadelphia *Bulletin* sought a baseball writer to replace Ray Kelly, a 35-year veteran of the beat who had just retired. Nobody on an excellent young sports staff wanted the assignment. The position was still unfilled midway through spring training. Mark Whicker, a brilliant new arrival from a newspaper in Dallas, was pulled off the NBA beat. He took the Phillies beat with great reservations, did an outstanding job through the 1980 season, and joyously bailed out when the sports columnist's job became vacant.

It goes on and on. The best and the brightest members of the sportswriting profession are bailing out of baseball press boxes as fast as they can pull the ripcords. The reasons are clear.

• During 1980 spring training at the Cubs' camp in Scottsdale, slugger Dave Kingman poured a tub of ice water over an unsuspecting writer from the Chicago suburbs. Very funny.

• In Cleveland, a veteran baseball writer, Russ Schneider, was assaulted by a manager while a coach pinned his arms behind him.

• In Baltimore, New York baseball writers Dick Young and Jack Lang had their clothing ruined when relief pitcher Eddie Watt doused them with a serving tray of barbecue sauce. Reason? Young and Lang had picked against the Orioles in a World Series.

• In Philadelphia, suburban writer Ray Kelly, Jr., was lured to the clubhouse by a "setup" pregame phone call and physically assaulted by Bowa, who didn't care for a critical column Kelly wrote. After the incident, club player representative Barry Foote gave the press a totally distorted account of what had happened.

• In Los Angeles in 1964, former Angels lefthander Bo Belinsky punched out baseball writer

Braven Dyer. Belinsky said Dyer came to his hotel room and took a swing at him. Dyer was in his sixties at the time.

• In Cincinnati, veteran baseball writer Earl Lawson was punched by all-star Reds outfielder Vada Pinson.

Literally scores of similar incidents in the last 15 years or so have gone unreported, covered up by club officials or by writers who didn't care to compromise their relationship with the rest of the players.

What the hell is going on here? Is this the profession that propelled Damon Runyon to greatness, the one which gave birth to literary giants like Ring Lardner and Paul Gallico?

It is the same, yet it is very different. The parameters of all sportswriting—indeed, all print journalism—have been blurred by the changes wrought by television's shattering immediacy, an immediacy driven home irrevocably the Sunday afternoon in 1963 when Lee Harvey Oswald was murdered by Jack Ruby, live and in living color. What could the ink-stained legends of the twenties and thirties do to counter the journalistic mismatch our technology had created?

As Dick Young graphically states in an interview later in this chapter, the new technology forced the sportswriter to get off his rear and find out what was really going on. No longer could a baseball writer sit in an ivory tower secure in the knowledge that his account of the game was the final word, no matter how fuzzy the focus or inaccurate the conclusions.

Fans had the basic details supplied over the airwaves with an immediacy newspapers could not hope to match, nor should they have tried to match it, because the one hammer the press still held was its ability to interpret in depth the events which the electronic disseminator could only skim from the changing surface of the world. Why? and how? became the salvation of the press, closely followed by, and in many cases superceded by, the question, "so what?"

Few of the established baseball writers measured up to the new demands and responsibilities thrust on them by the emergence of electronic journalism as a mighty rival. The great men of the twenties and thirties press boxes were for the most part stylists first and reporters second. The stylist can present a readable account of an event by interpreting what he sees. But the instant replay camera is graphic proof that the eye of the spectator is flawed, that the brain does not always retain or ac-

cept the message transmitted by the eye in the millisecond it takes for a baseball player to elude a tag, trap a short-hop in the outfield, or thrust a spiked shoe through a tiny sliver of daylight to gain an inch of a blocked home plate. The reporter must distrust his own perceptions, call himself a liar as it were, and pursue the unseen; he must reach beyond the obvious. And to accomplish this end, he must go among the athletes and supply the newspaper-reading public with a view of the game that even the replay camera fails to record.

In his clubhouse dealings, the skilled sports reporter must wear many faces because he is dealing with 25 men of different backgrounds, nationalities, races, and intellectual capacities, many of whom regard him and his probing questions with suspicion. He doesn't ask a rookie of limited education from a blinking-yellow-light-town in the South questions which require answers of great depth. Nor should he insult the many college-educated players in today's game with questions which can evoke only the obvious cliché.

The late Jimmy Cannon was a giant of sportswriting who commanded the respect of not only his peers, but of the New Wave sportswriters who came along in the sixties. An often lonely little man married to sportswriting for better or worse, Cannon was not an elegant essayist in the Red Smith mold; nor was he as skillful a reporter as Dick Young. But to read him was to touch a live wire with a wet hand. His prose crackled with a terse imagery ideal for the space strictures of a game story or column. Cannon could outrage you one day and have tears rolling down your cheeks the next. He was probably at his best reporting from boxing ringside, but his baseball pieces were consistently brilliant. He was an uncompromising critic who savaged the hypocrite and deflated the pompous.

In *No Cheering in the Press Box,* Jerome Holtzman's superbly recorded and edited classic of journalistic remembrances, Cannon said this about the role of the modern baseball writer:

"I don't agree with the delusion that a baseball writer is similar to the drama critic. The guys who cover the theater don't live with the actors and actresses. They don't travel with them on the same trains and the same planes and stay in the same hotels. They're not on the road with their subjects. I know some guys, career baseball writers, who say they've spent more time with ballplayers than with their own kids.

"The drama critic sits back and watches, like

we do, but he never goes backstage, or very rarely, and says, 'Why did you give a bad performance tonight?' The baseball writer goes to the losers after every game and demands that the athletes discuss their flaws. The baseball writer has it tough. . . . Professional ballplayers play for money and for fame. It's a tough hustle at the major league level. . . ."

And it is getting tougher. Free agency and long-term, megabuck contracts have changed the perception of how players view themselves and how they wish to be viewed by the press. One wedge a baseball writer always had prior to the death of the reserve clause was that no matter how important a player was—or how insignificant—his contract was always up at the end of the season. His future salary was in the hands of a flinty-eyed general manager hell bent on holding the line, determined to either increase the club's profits or keep losses to a minimum.

The player often had a scant knowledge of fiscal matters, and had no attorney or agent to advise him, or to at least serve as an adversarial flak-catcher in negotiations which frequently became hostile.

The baseball writer often became the unwitting middleman in the off-season ritual. "How about giving me some good ink?" a player would ask a writer during the dregs of September. "I'm having a lousy year, but I've driven in a lot of key runs. Maybe you could point that out in a story."

A writer would telephone an unsigned player during mid-winter to check on his status. "The old skinflint is trying to cut me twenty percent," the athlete would moan. "If I don't get a five-thousand-dollar raise I ain't reporting to spring training."

There it was, a nice holdout story to fuel the hot stove league.

The followup would be the general manager's response. "I tried to trade him but there's just no market for him. He can hold out until hell freezes over, as far as this ballclub is concerned. We've got some promising rookies who play his position, you know."

It was a timeless ritual, replayed so often that all the actors knew their lines by heart. After an appropriate amount of saber-rattling on both sides, they'd come to terms on the eve of spring training and the wire services would move a picture of a benevolent GM handing a blank contract to a smiling player holding a pen.

All that is history, as dead as vaudeville. Now, the player stays out of sight while attorneys in three-piece suits juggle mind-boggling figures and concoct contracts containing more clauses than the United States Constitution. The San Diego Padres wrote a clause into the 1980 contract of John Curtis, a journeyman lefthander, that he would be payed an additional $50,000 if he won the 1980 Cy Young award. Cy Young had a better chance to win it than John Curtis.

Having put the enormous pressure on themselves of earning sums of money far beyond the skill levels most of them possess, the players are suddenly confronted with the necessity of satisfying a public which expects every swing of the bat to produce a home run, every pitch to produce a strikeout. Being normal human beings who respond to praise and shrink from criticism, they do not take well to criticism of their performance by the press or paying fan.

Few possess the street-smart intelligence of a Pete Rose, who figures the right to boo poor performances comes with the price of a ticket.

"If a team or an individual plays lousy the fans ought to boo," Rose says. "It don't bother me. I just go out and try to do something that makes 'em cheer me instead. But a lot of players don't like it. Booing don't bother me."

Players tend to connect negative fan reaction with negative reviews in the press. In Philadelphia, where three consecutive division titles ended with the trauma of playoff elimination, "*Bleeping* negative Philadelphia sportswriters," has become a redundancy. "Philadelphia sportwriters," will do. The first part of the phrase is taken for granted.

Today's player—there are notable exceptions, of course—expects his good deeds to be lionized and his poor play ignored. He expects the baseball writers who cover him and his team to be an arm of the club's publicity department, cheerleaders. A slumping club should be encouraged by press support, not held up to ridicule.

There has been a proliferation in the past several years of players who do not speak to the press under any circumstances, even in an accidental meeting with a writer on a hotel elevator. Phillies' ace Steve Carlton, ex-Cubs' slugger Dave Kingman, and Cardinals' offensive star George Hendrick were the most prominent of the 1980 non-talkers. (It should be pointed out that not one newspaper folded as a result of their silence.)

When viewed through the eyes of a player, there is some justification for regarding the press with hostility and distrust. A player who has just participated in the key play of a shattering loss has

barely stripped off his uniform jersey when he is confronted by a considerable rabble of writers and tape recorder-wielding types from radio stations. In some of baseball's larger markets—New York, Philadelphia, Chicago, and Los Angeles—the number of accredited media members at an average game often exceeds 50. During a playoff and World Series, this number escalates past the 500 mark.

The player stands there, trapped within the confines of his locker space, and endures a dizzying barrage of questions, many of them banal, personal, and insulting. Some of the questions are fired by men and women he does not know by name or has never seen before, anonymous persons who nevertheless have the capacity to wound. He knows he runs the risk of having his words presented to the public out of context, invented outright, or twisted beyond recognition. If he is a player of stature, the chances are he has been burned before by sloppy, insensitive, or inaccurate reporting.

If he rewards the mob with a description of his play which includes a few one-liners, he will be considered a good copy. If he growls his answers, he will be depicted as "surly and uncooperative."

Unlike a pro football player who must endure the media mobs only once a week, a major league baseball player must stand before the grazing literati every day during a season which begins at a spring training site in late February and can extend to the third week of October.

And, whereas pro football and basketball players have been exposed to the press through their college careers, their baseball brethren are ill-prepared for mass interviews, or interviews of any kind. College baseball receives all the press coverage of church socials and there are few minor league towns where a player has to deal with more than a handful of press regulars. The majority of the game's raw material is still mined at the high school level, and most players who survive the weeding-out process have had scant preparation for the ordeal which lies ahead when they report to their first big league spring training camp. And those novitiates are swiftly influenced by the veteran players to treat the press with caution and distrust.

Players who would like to deal with writers they know and trust and writers who attempt to do their job with sensitivity and integrity are rare fellow travelers down a difficult, one-way street.

Dick Young's career as a baseball beat writer and columnist for the New York *Daily News* spans two eras. As a young, ambitious sportswriter on his first regular assignment covering the Dodgers in 1946, he broke long tradition by hurrying to the

In the glare of today's extensive media coverage, the streaks and slumps, brilliant plays and errors every player experiences, are examined minutely. Fans may plead for an autograph one day and boo the day after.

115

clubhouses after games to interview athletes involved in key plays. For decades, baseball writers had been content to tell their readers the "who" and "how" of games from a subjective point of view. Young made a habit of telling "why," adding in a terse, irreverent style an occasional, "so what?"

Young has fought zealously over the years for rights of free access to players before and after games, rights which have been gradually eroded to the point where it is increasingly difficult for the press to fulfill its function.

I interviewed Dick Young at the 1980 winter baseball meetings in Dallas just minutes after he had made his stirring yearly appeal for free access during the annual meeting of the Baseball Writers Association of America.

Q—What were press-player relations like when you started covering the Dodgers in 1946?

Young—It was just great. Maybe part of that was because I was the same age as many of the ballplayers, although I don't think that was the entire explanation. I don't see the same intimacy today between young writers and ballplayers that I saw in my time, when I was actually running with the ballplayers.

Q—Considering the atmosphere of veiled and sometimes open contempt in fashion today, that's hard to believe. Were relationships really that close?

Young—Yeah, they were my friends. I'm not saying it was an idyllic relationship because we had our differences at times. If you're going to do a good job in the newspaper business, you're going to have to be critical. I won't say they were as sensitive as they are today, at least not manifestly. Once in a while they would get annoyed at something and make a crack like, "Get the f--- away from me," but they'd get over it. In a hurry. In fact, Pee Wee Reese had a philosophy where he'd say, "If I have a bad day I don't read the newspapers because I don't want to get mad at anybody." Which is a pretty good philosophy.

Q—Baseball writing practice was pretty well established by 1946. Why did you break with tradition and start going to the clubhouse for postgame quotes?

Young—I just thought it was interesting if there was a controversial play in a game or something similar that needed explanation. If I couldn't understand why a player didn't do a certain thing I would go down to the clubhouse and ask him. It was that simple. I thought it was just an integral part of the story. The older writers didn't like that much. It was pretty much a handout era where the guys would sit up in the press box with a release from the ballclub and write what they saw. In fact, one writer used to say, "I don't have to go down and talk to the players. I know what I'm looking at." In other words, a pontificating attitude. Of course, there's no justification for that. I don't know why, but nobody did it any differently. I don't know how they got away with it. I guess you could get away with anything if everybody was doing the same thing.

Q—Did the way you worked have a snowballing effect? It would seem that in those days, the fans were pretty much a captive audience.

Young—There was radio, of course. But all they needed was one newspaperman to break it down. As soon as one did, the others had to do it. That's why I wasn't too popular at the time, because some of the guys had to get off their ass and go downstairs, too. But getting back to the closeness that prevailed. We lived with them more, particularly on the railroad trains. There's nothing in my mind like a poker game to make fellows understand each other. You're either going to know if a guy's no good or you're going to get to like him in a poker game. It's a very deep character revelation. There was an awful lot of poker being played in those days. You'd have dinner with the ballplayers in the diner. As soon as you'd finish dinner somebody would say, "Let's have a card game." And you'd take the dirty dishes away and put a green cloth on the table and start the poker game and it would go on for hours and hours.

I remember in 1946, which was my first regular year on the beat, the Dodgers finished the regular season tied with the Cardinals, the first time in history there was a pennant tie, a playoff involving a tie. We went from Brooklyn to St. Louis to Brooklyn, best out of three. St. Louis won and entered the World Series against Boston, so it was back to St. Louis, back to Boston, back to St. Louis. In those days it was the longest trip you could make in baseball, well over a day—twenty-four hours, twenty-six hours. The poker games went on like crazy and you really got to know each other. It does help, compared to not traveling at all, because they get to see you and they get to trust you a little more when you are a traveling guy as opposed to a guy they just see standing around the batting cage.

I believe in traveling with the club. It gives you access. It is nothing now compared to what it was

The impact of sudden visibility on a young player can be significant. He has to concentrate on his job in front of 30,000 fans, TV cameras, and scores of media types who come up to him after the game to ask, "Why?"

117

in the days of the railroad trains.

Q—Can you put a finger on the adversarial relationship that seems to have escalated so much in the past five years or so?

Young—We don't know each other and, therefore, we don't trust each other as much. I think the union (Players Association) has a lot to do with it. The ballplayers feel their muscle in the union. They used to be a little bit insecure, or relatively so. A player almost *had* to be nice to you, even if it wasn't to his advantage to be friendly to a newspaper guy. Now they feel they don't need anybody. They're running the show. Dave Kingman had a famous line to Don Grant when he was with the Mets and they were talking a contract: "You don't realize, Mr. Grant, things have changed. We're in the driver's seat now. We're calling the shots." That's a pretty general attitude, although I don't think anybody is as brazen about it as Dave Kingman. But they all have that idea that it's pretty much their game and they're going to have things pretty much their own way. They know they can file a grievance if they don't like something.

Q—Has television's emergence as a super-medium diminished the impact a baseball writer once had?

Young—I'm not aware there's been any diminution. The public realizes that the integrity of the press is entirely different than the integrity of television, and I don't wish to demean TV in a blanket sense. I know some very fine radio and TV people. But the very nature of their business, where they are actually in a partnership with the sports promoter, necessitates a different relationship than ours. We are as objective as anybody can get—again I'm generalizing; nothing is one hundred percent. We still are right down the middle of the road, where we should be. We don't have an ax to grind.

We don't have any profit to take, whereas the other guys are pretty much subject to censorship, economic or otherwise, by the sports promoter, by the owner. I think the public realizes that. We do have a respect that the other guys don't have. We do have a credibility that they don't have. A lot of people in TV are aware of that. One thing that bugs me about Howard Cosell, for instance, and why he keeps referring to himself as a journalist—which is a joke—is because he feels we have a credibility he

President Jimmy Carter and Speaker of the House Tip O'Neill chat with Major League Baseball Commissioner Bowie Kuhn at the 1980 World Series. All presidents know the importance of baseball, hotdogs, and apple pie.

doesn't have. Maybe not as much money, but a credibility. A little personal quirk, if I may interject it, is that I hate the word "media," because it blankets us with them. And I say "press." We are the press. Let them use their own word.

Q—What do you see down the road for relations between the press and the baseball establishment in general and the players in particular?

Young—I think we must be on guard with an eternal vigilance to protect our working rights. We must keep our rights from being eroded day, by day, by day. The promoters will pander to television and they will give them extra access and favors. I'm not trying to stop them from getting things because it's good for the fan to get as much as he can. But I want equal access. I don't want to have to compete at a disadvantage. I don't think it's fair and I don't think it's right.

Q—Can we go full cycle? Will diminished access and hostile player attitudes force the press back to the days of pontificating, the drama critic school of writing?

Young—It's always a danger. We have a situation where we used to stay in the clubhouse right up to game time. I've stood in dugouts while the national anthem was being played and sung it with the ballplayers before racing upstairs to the press box to see the first pitch. You can't do that anymore.

You must be out of there regardless of whether it's fifteen minutes or forty-five minutes. In some instances, some guys don't let you in the clubhouse at all after the game. And that is a real danger because I find myself saying if I have another choice maybe I'll go to another event today. As a columnist, my interest is in talking to people before the game and after the game. If I'm cut off from the source of information, I've got another event to go to, a basketball game, or soccer game, whatever. That is something baseball better become aware of; they're still in competition with other sports.

Q—Some papers are having trouble filling the baseball beat with top men. In some cases, they're almost shanghaiing writers. Do you see a trend developing where the baseball beat is no longer the glamour job it once was?

Young—Yes. The plum assignment on every newspaper was the baseball beat. It used to be that guys waited for the baseball writer to die and inherit the job because it was pleasant to cover. It was interesting, it was all-day ball and all the elements made it the choice assignment. Now, you have to really love it to have to do it. You don't have that

many young fellows loving it, so they come in and either pass on to some other sport or they quit the newspaper business. They don't have any real feeling for it. Some people still think that we're stealing money, that we're paid to watch ball games. They don't realize that there's an awful lot of aggravation involved in it, and that you do put in tremendous hours, especially if you work for a morning paper. If we are forced into it, as human beings we take the course of least resistance. You fight it for a while and then you say, "What the hell am I knocking myself out for? I'm fighting for a principle that nobody else appreciates. Why don't I just take the money and run?"

I hope it doesn't come to that. There will always be some decent players around. I must add the public relations is the property of management and that property is being usurped by the Players Association and managers who play footsie with their ballplayers. Why ownership permits managers to put in rules which favor the ballplayers when publicity is so valuable to management I'll never understand. Clubs that are making it now couldn't care less. That's another facet of human nature. When the Mets came along and had to compete with the Yankees, the Mets couldn't do enough for the writers. There were no restrictions. We could have gone on the field during the game and Casey Stengel would have said, "Come on down." Once the Mets won the pennant the whole scene changed.

Q—The economy is shaky right now, to say the least. Would attitudes change toward the press if there were a major economic disruption?

Young—I would think it could come tumbling down in no time at all with a decent depression. Art Rooney once said to NFL owners, "Gentlemen, we're taking too much money for our TV rights, and we are basing our whole economy on that television money. Someday that money's going to be snapped away from us and the whole structure's going to come tumbling down." It's tough to take back what you've given away, but it can happen. Before the Great Depression a lot of workers were making a hundred dollars a week. Then the plant owners would come and say, "If we're going to keep this plant open, you're going to have to accept a cut in wages." So now, people were making fifty dollars a week and finally the hundred-dollars-a-week man was making thirty-five and damn glad to get it. All it would take is a moderate downward revision in the TV money to bring the whole baseball economy tumbling down.

8

8

A Week in the Life

A baseball player whose career spans 10 years in the major leagues will spend a startling amount of time away from wherever he calls home. He will spend a total of 14 months at a spring training site. The good news there is that his family will probably be with him. Spring training has long been a family affair and many ballclub people—including front office executives and media types—wind up retiring in the Sun Belt resort where they spent so many months during their careers.

The 10-year man will spend a total of three regular season months in each city in his team's division and two months in the cities of the other division. Counting open dates on the road, exhibitions with minor league teams during the regular season and spring training, he will be living from a suitcase an average of 4.1 months each year between the last week in February and first week in October. Much of that time will be spent in the air on commercial or charter flights, or on the ground in buses provided to take him between airports and hotels, hotels and ballparks. In 10 years, he will spend approximately 1,000 hours in the air, flying jets which will carry him close to one million miles. He will spend about 1,250 hours—the equivalent of 52 days—riding the team bus.

During this staggering chunk of time out of what is already an abnormal existence, his wife will be left alone to raise the children and wrestle with the loneliness, suspicions, and potential jealousies indigenous to "army" wives. Her husband will be subjected to a disconcerting level of recognition and accompanying temptations. His moral fiber will be severely tested almost every day of his road career. Even if he lives by the Boy Scout oath—and few players do—temptations lurk at every turn.

Yet a surprisingly high percentage of baseball marriages survive, despite the imposing odds against them. The baseball widow is a hearty species, wise to the ways of the world. Many met their husbands in some kind of social, road situation. They know what kind of jungle it is out there and the nature of the predators who prowl it. And although they do not sanction infidelity, many accept the possibility with a stoic loyalty.

There are other temptations. A player of the drinking persuasion can swiftly fall into a morass of alcoholism. Beer is the staple beverage of every clubhouse and the postgame retreat to a watering hole a time-honored ritual. Despite scare stories you read from time to time about drug abuse, use of recreational drugs—grass, speed, and cocaine—is at a no higher percentage than among affluent "civilians" in the 20- to 40-year-old age group. In the fifties and sixties, amphetamines were so widely available in clubhouses from baseball trainers it would have been a major scandal if anybody in those days had known the true nature of "speed." There is far less amphetamine use now and no club makes "greenies" available.

Potential family breakups, the dangers of alcohol or drug abuse, and the mind-bending demands of constant travel are the negative aspects of a 162-game schedule played over a six-month span in cities hundreds and sometimes thousands of miles apart. But for the average young man with the common sense to see through all the bull and who can adapt to the harsh demands of travel, the road can be terrific. Unlike his National Basketball Association brethren, who are truly gypsies living a series of one-night stands in winter towns, he has the opportunity to see America in summer, explore great restaurants, live in first-class hotels, visit vineyards and famed golf courses, see Broadway shows and the glitter of Hollywood. As Tim McCarver, a well-traveled catcher, said as he reached his thirty-sixth birthday, "I don't think I can take this life more than another twenty years."

What's it really like out there? Let's spend a 1980 week in California with the Philadelphia Phillies—in diary form:

San Francisco, Monday, September 1

The Pope is hopping mad. You could fry an egg on his forehead. For those of you who don't know him, The Pope is Paul Owens, the Phillies GM, and last night he just about took apart the Airport Hilton. Owens watched the Padres beat the Phillies 10–3 in San Diego yesterday and he hasn't stopped reading the riot act since. Herm Starrette, the folksy pitching coach, says he ran into The Pope in the lobby last night and asked him something innocuous like, "How you doin'?" Paul's reply was, "Who the bleep wants to know?"

Much of his anger stems from two fly balls Garry Maddox lost in the sun during yesterday's horror show. It turns out Maddox had his sunglasses in his back pocket and didn't bother to put them on. Garry went to Dallas Green, the manager, and offered to apologize to the club.

Green said that wouldn't be necessary, for Maddox to just go out and do what he's getting paid to do. But writers were betting Maddox would be benched and they were right.

So here it is, Labor Day, and the Phillies are in first place. Owens called a clubhouse meeting before the game that left blistered paint. When you're going to lecture the troops it helps to have your best pitcher going—just in case. Steve Carlton didn't have his best stuff, but he beat the drag-ass Giants, 6–4, for his twenty-first victory. Back at the hotel, the players are still talking about The Pope's clubhouse performance and you can bet there won't be many guys out on the town tonight. Room service figures to do a land-office business.

It seems strange to be stuck out here next to the east-west runway of a major airport in a city as good as San Francisco, but that's what the athletes wanted. They rate The City near the bottom and why not? Athletes are not lionized here the way they are in New York or Los Angeles. Baseball players are mostly steak-and-potato men, so they don't take advantage of the great restaurants here. They'd just as soon eat at Phil Lehr's than the Blue Fox or La Bourgogne. Although they complain about the hassle of being famous, ballplayers seem to resent it when they are completely unrecognized and ignored. Hell, Willie Mays had to completely alter his batting style and hit 52 home runs to gain any recognition in this town, one of the most provincial in the country despite a reputation for sophistication that is largely a myth. There isn't a single bar in town that caters to ballplayers and ballplayers hate to go out to the Union Street Meet Markets and mingle with the civilians.

Anyway, The Pope shouted the Phils into first place today and it appears the townsfolk for now at least are safe.

San Francisco, Tuesday, September 2

They've had a cold summer here and today is no exception, gray and drizzly with a cigar-shaped roll of fog hanging on the Twin Peaks section and jagged patches scudding through Downtown. It's hard to see how a player can put in a season playing in Candlestick Park, let alone a career. The weather will be brutal out there tonight. When the fog doesn't burn off by early afternoon, the wind is guaranteed to howl. It's supposed to be the Summer Game, but in this town baseball is a game of eternal London November. The weather is only a little better on the east side of the bay, but the Oakland A's get their share of raw, windy nights.

For the athletes, San Diego is a poolside town. Los Angeles is a shopping town. The City is a town where players tend to go to the park early and play cards or backgammon. You'd be amazed at how many hours players spend at the yard. The team bus leaves the hotel two and a half hours before game time. Only a handful of players ride it most days. The rest go out earlier, some as early as 3 P.M. before a night game. Some take extra hitting practice. Others sit around in their long johns and read the papers. The walking-wounded are always out early for treatment from trainers Don Seger and Jeff Cooper, who usually arrive by one o'clock. Anybody who says you can't beat baseball's hours is crazy. Seger, Cooper, and Kenny Bush, the clubhouse manager, log an average of 12 hours a day at the ballpark on the road, even more on getaway days when they have to pack the equipment.

Baseball's fringe people don't get enough credit. The average fan figures all the coaches do is hit fungos during batting and infield practice. Or shag balls and holler, "Attababy."

Billy DeMars, the Phillies' batting coach, is another workaholic who goes to the ballpark early. Long before the team bus arrives, Billy has already put in a full day of work, pitching batting practice in a cage under the stands to a slumping hitter, studying miles of videotape film in slow motion to find a faulty stride here, a head pulling off the ball there. Like many clubs, the Phils employ a full-time photographer who films every at bat of every game and every pitch thrown by the pitching staff. Baseball finally learned from big time football that you really don't know anything until you've seen the films.

Another tireless worker who can be found at the ballpark hours early is Gus Hoefling, hired as the club's fitness and strength director. Not every player is into his demanding program, but he works with about a dozen athletes, including Steve Carlton and Bob Boone. Carlton and Boone subscribe to his total program, which includes brutal stretching exercises, Nautilus workouts, and a high-level martial arts curriculum. Hoefling estimates that Boone has made a more than 150 percent gain in efficient strength. Carlton was a brute before he became a Hoefling disciple and now his strength and endurance are awesome. At 35, Carlton is stronger, more flexible, and injury free than he was at 21. It's eerie stuff and more and more teams will be getting into it. Strange that it took baseball almost 75 years to realize that the playing of the game itself is not enough to keep an athlete in condition. Compare the energy an NBA player expends in 35 minutes of play with what a baseball player expends in nine innings. It's no contest. Which reminds me of something Gene Mauch once told me, "The only muscle a baseball player can tire consistently is his brain."

Very true. The mentally fatigued Phils went out and beat the Giants again tonight and got another well-pitched game from Dick Ruthven. Two days in first place. Unbelievable.

San Francisco, Wednesday, September 3

One of these days there will be a riot on a commercial airplane. It won't be caused by a bomb-toting terrorist or a two-hour equipment delay. It will be caused by a harried businessman on standby who is denied a seat on a plane which will take off with at least eight empty seats.

Sound like Catch 22? Yes. Someday it will happen. The airline agent will try to explain to this foaming-at-the-mouth type that even though the empty seats are physically there, they are theoretically occupied, thanks to the existing Basic Agreement between the Major League Players Association and the owners. One of the agreement's stipulations is that all players will fly first class whenever possible. Well, most first-class compartments have been reduced to maybe 8 seats, which leaves 17 players back in coach. To ameliorate their suffering back in steerage, the owners agreed to purchase one seat extra for each two players forced to ride in the back of the plane, so there would be an empty seat between players. Thus a club with 17 players seated in coach would be forced to buy 9 extra tickets. With airlines cutting back schedules, many flights between major cities are operating near capacity. More than one spurned standby passenger has gone storming off a flight with a negative impression of big league baseball teams.

Tired of the fog and gloom on this side of the Bay, Mark Whicker, the Philadelphia *Bulletin* baseball writer, and I decide to make a mini wine tour. In just under an hour, we're over the Golden Gate Bridge, past Sausalito and Mill Creek, and deep into Sonoma County, where it is 80 degrees under a cloudless blue sky. We tour the Buena Vista winery, the first in California, founded by the legendary Count Agostin Haraszthy.

We spend an hour in the tasting room and wind up buying a full-bodied 1976 Cabernet, a sensitive 1977 Pinot Chardonnay, and Buena Vista's Gold Medal-winning 1978 Zinfandel, a spicy red filled with mystery. Then on to lunch in Sonoma at a delightful deli-teria a stone's throw from the mission-style building which was California's first state capitol. A lot of baseball players are into fine wines and many of them make winery tours each year. Steve Carlton even made an expensive off-season pilgrimage to the great vineyards of France one season. That's nice. A man can't live by fastballs alone.

The athletes are over the Owens tirade by now. So is The Pope, who is joking about his performance. There's a charged atmosphere in the clubhouse, but it has nothing to do with tonight's game with the Giants. When you play every day it's not easy to look ahead, but the Phillies are looking ahead to the big four-game series in Los Angeles. The Dodgers are battling the Astros in the West, the Phils are clinging to first place in the East. It will be one of those rare series where first place in two divisions will be at stake. After playing before 6,000 half-frozen fans in this forbidding, fortress of a ballpark, Dodger Stadium will be like heaven— 45,000 people in the stands. Sinatra and Rickles in their box seats. Cary Grant holding forth with his lovely daughter in the O'Malleys' VIP booth. Dodger baseball is tinged with show biz, but anything beats Candlestick Park, the National League's Alcatraz.

Los Angeles, Thursday, September 4

The Screen Actors Guild is still on strike, but there was no scarcity of play-acting in Dodger Stadium tonight. Tug McGraw, about as popular here as the Hillside Strangler, showed up for batting practice wearing a Marine camouflage shirt and a khaki helmet liner of Korean War vintage. Bill Russell, the Dodgers shortstop, came out on the field wearing giant boxing gloves.

Some background: During the last L.A.-Phillies series back East, McGraw was in the process of issuing an intentional walk to catcher Joe Ferguson, normally a nonviolent baseball event. But Ferguson outraged McGraw by sticking his bat out at one of Tug's waste pitches and lining it to right for a single. The next hitter was Russell. Still simmering over the Ferguson fiasco, McGraw threw three pitches inside to Russell and drilled him with the fourth. The shortstop charged the mound and both benches emptied for the obligatory brawl.

Tug's crazy like a fox. His military getup broke the crowd tension and he and Russell shook hands on Stu Nahan's pregame TV show.

But the night belonged to Bob Walk, a Phillies' rookie righthander who was raised in the nearby San Fernando Valley. There's a story there, too. The last time Walk appeared in Dodger Stadium he was in the left field bleachers, drinking beer and raising hell with the rest of the crazies. It was 1974 and Walk was kicked out of the park for throwing a tennis ball at Houston outfielder Cesar Cedeno. Somehow, as the security guards led Bob to the parking lot, he knew he would be back to play a larger role than that of a disorderly person. And tonight, Bob shut out the Dodgers until the eighth inning, when the kid ran out of gas. Warren Brusstar was batted around for two runs and the Phillies were suddenly clinging to a 3–2 lead. McGraw, (who else?), survived a ninth inning jam and got the save when Tommy Lasorda sent up Manny Mota, the recently activated first base coach and pinch-hitting legend. Manny received a rousing ovation from the huge crowd, but he bounced feebly to short and the Phillies had a one-game lead over the Expos and Pirates in what is turning into a ding-dong race. Even jaded sportswriters are excited about tomorrow night's matchup—Steve Carlton versus Don Sutton. I'd almost pay to watch that duel. Almost.

Los Angeles, Friday, September 5

Hotels are important when you're on the road as much as a major league baseball team. Most members of the traveling party rank the Wilshire-Hyatt here near the top of the list. It's not as swank as the Shamrock Hilton in Houston or a total resort like the Town and Country in San Diego, two other favorites. It's just a medium-size first-class hotel in the Wilshire Center, right up the boulevard from the Ambassador, where Robert F. Kennedy was shot. It's not particularly convenient to anything. Dodger Stadium is 25 minutes away. It's 40 minutes in heavy traffic to the tony shops of Beverly Hills' Rodeo Drive and 45 minutes to an hour by freeway to Marina Del Rey and the Santa Monica area beaches.

The Wilshire-Hyatt's superb staff makes the difference. It's nice to check into a hotel where everybody from the doorman to Rosemary, the pleasant lady who runs the Carnival Lounge, knows you on a first-name basis. Nor is there any phony bowing or scraping. The Phillies have stayed here since 1968 and a warm relationship has developed over the years, a relationship so spontaneous that the cocktail waitresses who staff the lounge come to work the day the team checks in wearing Phillies T-shirts and caps without being told. Contrast that with the New York-Sheraton, where a smile or hello may be hard won.

It's low-key in the Carnival Lounge tonight, though, with a lot of serious baseball talk going on. Sutton cranked up his best performance of the season to beat Carlton, 1–0, in a duel that exceeded expectations. Carlton made just one mistake. He hung a breaking ball to Ron Cey in the fourth and the stumpy third baseman drove it into the bleachers in left center. The Phillies never came close to scoring. Sutton worked the corners with consummate artistry. There was no need for an angry clubhouse meeting tonight. It's tough to grind it out when you can't get on base.

Los Angeles, Saturday, September 6

Thank God, it's Saturday. That means my newspaper doesn't publish a Sunday edition and I'm free to prove that L.A. really is a great big freeway. But even though I had lunch at a terrific place in Marina Del Rey, nothing will top the two days I spent in Mexico last weekend. The first day, a friend and I did the Baja beach and restaurant tour—lunch at the Rosaritia Beach Hotel, cocktails at the legendary pit, Hussong's Cantina in Ensenada, and mouth-watering sautéed abalone at a seaside restaurant in Playa Ensenada about four kilometers south of the city. Sunday it was back down to Tijuana for the bullfights at the Bullring by the Sea. The *corridas* were bush league—bad bulls and worse matadors. But it was a trip doing the Ugly American number, à la Errol Flynn in *The Sun Also Rises.* Much cheap wine and tequila.

The ballplayers miss out on a lot when they travel. They're not allowed to play golf or tennis during the season. It's tough to do much serious touring when you don't get to bed until 2 A.M. and have to leave for the yard no later than 5 P.M. At least managers have dropped the old restriction on ballplayers swimming. For years, swimming was forbidden in season as an exercise that tightened up the muscles, which is nonsense, of course. In the Sun Belt towns—San Diego, Los Angeles, Houston, Atlanta, and St. Louis—the swimming pool gets even more action than the hotel bar.

The hotel bar . . . That's another area of divided baseball opinion. Many clubs put the hotel bar off limits for players, which means they will merely do their drinking someplace else. The more progressive view is to let the athletes drink where they please. The hotel bar promotes a certain camaraderie and the Phillies have had no problems whatsoever with that approach.

One thing is certain. The road is expensive. The ballclub gets very attractive rates from its headquarters hotels, ranging from about $30 a night in Houston to $78 a night (in 1981) at the Union Square Hyatt in San Francisco, a convention town where clubs have had a difficult time achieving permanency. In 1981, meal money will be raised to $37.50 a day. Nobody can eat three meals in a hotel or decent restaurant for that money. What "meal money" really is is walking-around money. You buy breakfast or lunch, eat a free meal at the ballpark. The balance may or may not be enough to buy a round of drinks. With drinks in Montreal's Regency Hyatt averaging about four dollars, there are not many nights when a player is tempted to set up the bar, even the rich players.

Los Angeles, Sunday, September 7

Getaway Day! The end of a three-city, 10-game trip. The athletes are weary—physically and mentally. They were 6–2 after the first game here, but the well has run dry. You could see the offense going to sleep when Sutton shut them out Friday night. Now, they have lapsed into a numbing team batting slump. The slump, an equal opportunities employer, got the Bad Housekeeping Seal of Approval today. Two mediocrities, overpaid free agent Dave Goltz, and undistinguished reliever Rudy Castillo, beat the Phils 6–0 in an incredibly drab game.

The club is silent and somber on the long haul through weekend traffic down the Santa Monica and San Diego Freeways to LAX. We've got a charter and that's a break. They'll start loosening up about halfway through the five-hour flight, but right now there are no stereos blaring, no barracks humor.

The plane will land about 2 A.M. By the time the buses get to Veterans Stadium and the players collect their luggage it will be close to three o'clock.

The same scene is being repeated all over baseball. Sunday is almost always a travel day. The Phillies are one of the few teams that are still alive. By this stage of September, the contenders are down to a precious few. For the teams fighting to stay in first place or overtake the leaders, there will be no time to nurse bruises, study films, and formulate a fresh game plan.

The Phillies will be back at the ballpark in less than 14 hours, ready to battle their Eastern Division archenemy, the Pirates.

It is an early morning hour of September 8, 1980. The Summer Game is moving toward its climactic autumn phase and the long season still has six more weeks to run before a World Series champion is crowned.

Left: *Hitters use the batting cage throughout the season.* Above: *Ultimately, it is a player's self-discipline that drives him to excel. Daily workouts and practices are simply reflections of commitment.*

Credits
All photographs included in this book were
taken by the photographers of FOCUS ON SPORTS,
222 East 46th Street, New York, New York 10017,
with the exception of page 16, by
UNITED PRESS INTERNATIONAL.